Teaching
Strings

Teaching Strings

Learning to Teach through Playing

SECOND EDITION

ROBERT H. KLOTMAN

SCHIRMER BOOKS
An Imprint of Simon & Schuster Macmillan
NEW YORK

Prentice Hall International
LONDON   MEXICO CITY   NEW DELHI   SINGAPORE   SYDNEY   TORONTO

Schirmer Books
An Imprint of Simon & Schuster Macmillan
1633 Broadway
New York, NY 10019

Library of Congress Catalog Card No.: 96-10607

Printed in the United States of America

printing number
1 2 3 4 5 6 7 8 9 10

Library of Congress Cataloging-in-Publication Data

Klotman, Robert H.
    Teaching strings : learning to teach through playing / Robert H.
  Klotman. — 2nd ed.
        p.   cm.
    Includes bibliographical references and index.
    ISBN 0-02-864579-0 (alk. paper)
    1. Stringed instruments, Bowed—Instruction and study. I. Title.
  MT259.K58 1996
787'.07—dc20   96–10607
                                                                            CIP
                                                                            MN

Excerpts from Phyllis Young, *Playing the String Games: Strategies for Teaching Cello and Strings,*
© 1978 by the University of Texas Press, have been reprinted here by permission of the publisher and the author.

The example of scordatura tuning from Richard Felciano, "O He Did Whistle and She Did
Sing," © 1972 by E. C. Schirmer Music Co., Inc., Boston, has been reprinted here by permission
of the publisher.

This paper meets the requirements of ANSI/NISO Z39.48–1992 (Permanence of Paper).

*Dedicated to the memory of ERNEST E. HARRIS,
adviser, colleague, collaborator, and friend.*

Contents

Songs and Literature

Acknowledgments

The author wishes to express gratitude and appreciation to the following contributors who have allowed use of their materials:

The American String Teachers Association, Robert Cowden, Publications Chair

Edward Campbell, luthier, The Chimneys Violin Shop

Walter Coplin, teacher of string bass, West Virginia University

Peter Horn, Horn and Son Stringed Instruments

Heinrich Roth, past president of Scherl and Roth Company

Kent Miller and Nick Judy, photographers, Indiana University Audio-Visual Center

Marianne Murray Perkins, George Mason University

Sketches by Marvin Lowe, Professor Emeritus of Fine Arts, Indiana University

and to the following individuals who posed for the illustrations:

Stella Anderson, viola/violin instructor, MacPhail Center for the Arts, Minneapolis

Sara Caswell, violin student, College for Gifted and Talented Youth, Indiana University

Cory Cerovsek, violin student, Indiana University

Darin Chertkoff, cellist, College for Gifted and Talented Youth, Indiana University

Simone Gubar, cellist, College for Gifted and Talented Youth, Indiana University

William Koehler, professor of string bass, Illinois State University, who also assisted with the editing

and to those who have assisted with the section on materials in this book:

Jody Atwood, director, advertising and promotions, Warner Bros. Publications, Inc.

Diana Rogers Elledge, editor of string music, Neil A. Kjos Music Company, Publishers

Lawrence Hurst, professor of double bass, chair of the String Department, School of Music, Indiana University

Elizabeth A. Levin, orchestra/strings director, Southport Public Schools, Indianapolis

Stanton's Sheet Music, Columbus, Ohio

Preface

The preparation of string teachers has an interesting history. There have been several approaches in general practice. The early, so-called methods courses for the preparation of teachers of instrumental music placed stress on the lecture system. The expectation was that the college teacher would explain the principles and practices, and the student would read about the subject and possibly observe some actual teaching situations where these methods were applied in the classroom.

Another prevalent view is that the best preparation for teachers of instruments or groups of instruments lies in the acquisition of as much skill as possible in the actual playing of the instrument. The theory here is simply that one should be able to do what one is attempting to teach others to do. In this approach the usual pattern is to teach the future teacher to play the instrument involved, using the same material that young students will use. Certainly one of the strongest objections to this idea is that the college-level student, a somewhat mature adult, has been forced to spend too much time with musical literature at a far more immature level than is justified.

In recent years educators have come to recognize that students in higher education should have material especially designed for their level of musical maturity, even as they are acquiring knowledge about elementary instrumental performance. Most of the publications thus far either have emphasized the verbalization of method—in which case there is insufficient musical material for full realization of the principle involved—or else have consisted primarily of music to be played, without sufficient explanation of concepts, principles, and practices. This textbook integrates musical material with minimum but essential verbalization.

The text seeks to provide a broad view of the total string-instruction program in a well-planned sequence for the training of the future string teacher. It includes references to the preschool child, as exemplified in the Suzuki approach, action and body-motion studies as advocated by Paul Rolland, and rote-to-note practices.

To guide the student through the text, clearly stated objectives—indicated as *competencies*—are provided throughout. These competency standards were selected through analysis of the skills required by a beginning teacher for organizing and teaching string classes of young people. They are arranged sequentially, so that as students move through each level of competency, they will develop the skills essential for teaching strings.

Another feature of this book is the provision for student self-evaluation. Self-check lists throughout identify activities for each level of competency so that students may check their progress themselves.

PART 1

General Information Regarding String Instruments

Construction and Nomenclature

| Competency 1: | Be able to name the various parts of the body of the string instruments, back and front. |
| Competency 1.1: | Be able to name the various parts of the bow. |

Construction of String Instruments

The best string instruments are made from wood. In the interest of the financial constraints on school budgets and the grueling use that many instruments receive, some acceptable substitute materials have been developed. Under no circumstances, however, should substitutes be used if they distort tonal images and basic musical sound.

The tops of string instruments are usually made of even, narrow-grained spruce. The head, the neck, the sides or ribs, and the bridge are made of various grades of maple. The nut, the fingerboard, the saddle, and the inlaid purfling should be made of ebony. The pegs, tail-piece, and end button are usually ebony, but they may also be rosewood or boxwood.

Chin rests will vary. They may be made of ebony, rosewood, boxwood, or a plastic. The best end pins are made of steel and should be adjustable. The string bass has mechanical, geared pegs. These should be mounted on a brass plate.

One of the acceptable substitutes may be laminated wood, sometimes used for the top, back, and sides of cellos or basses; it should be carefully checked for quality. Fiberglass basses have been found to be most economical and quite satisfactory for school use.

Identifying the materials and parts of string instruments

The finish should be of high-quality, polished varnish. Lacquer is not acceptable for string instruments.

BOWS

The better bows are made of Pernambuco wood. A good quality brazil-wood may be an adequate substitute, but under no circumstances should one accept beechwood. Fiberglass bows have proved extremely satisfactory for school use.

Nomenclature of String Instruments

All string instruments use the same nomenclature for their various parts. Since cellos and basses rest on the floor, they have additional items, such as an end pin and adjusting screw that keeps the end pin in place. (Naturally there is no chin rest on the cello or bass.) To prevent sliding, these instruments should utilize a stop of some sort or find a hole in the floor where the end pin may be inserted to provide stability.

It is important that the string teacher be able to identify the parts by their correct terms, since these are the common language of string players.

In addition, using correct terms prevents misunderstanding when requesting repairs by mail or phone. As obvious as this advice seems, there is a disconcerting amount of confusion created when conventional terms are not used.

Scroll
Peg
Peg-box
Nut
Fingerboard
Neck
Top
Ribs (Bouts)
Purfling
F Hole
Bridge
Tuner
Tailpiece
Chin rest
Saddle
Tailpiece Gut
Button

Figure 1–1

Figure 1–1 shows a front exterior view of the parts of a violin or viola; Figure 1–2 shows the rear exterior of a string bass. (When comparing a violin and viola, note that the viola is slightly larger in all dimensions.) Figure 1–3 shows a cross section of the interior.

Neck block

Back

Purfling

Adjusting screw
End pin

Figure 1–2

Bass bar
(under the bass strings)

Rib lining

Sound post

Neck block

End block

Figure 1–3

Figure 1–4

French   German

Figure 1–5

The Bow

The nomenclature for the bow is the same for each member of the string family (see Fig. 1–4). The parts of the bow for each instrument vary in size and thickness in proportion to the length of the stick.

The only instrument with two styles of bow is the string bass, which may be played with either a French- or German-style ("Butler") bow (see Fig. 1–5). However, the French conforms to the bows of the other members of the string family and is the more popular in most string classes.

> ### Activities and Check List
>
> 1. Select a string instrument and name each part as you point to it.
> 2. Select a violin, viola, or violoncello bow and name each part as you point to it.
> 3. Describe the distinguishing features of the French- and German-style bass bows. Indicate by pointing to the different parts.
> 4. Indicate the distinguishing features among the violin, viola, and violoncello bows (length and thickness).
> 5. Describe the materials that are used in the construction of string instruments and their various accessories. (See pp. 3, 8, and 9.)

Extended Range of the String Family

Beginning with the lowest note on the string bass to the highest note on the violin, the string choir of the orchestra spans a range of over six octaves. (Incidentally, the string bass sounds one octave lower than where it is written.)

Care and Maintenance of String Instruments

> Competency 2: Be able to identify the rules for care and repair that apply to all string instruments.

A careful program of preventive maintenance can save much time and prevent unnecessary abuses and damage that lead to costly repairs.

A few simple rules that apply to all string instruments are as follows:

1. After each playing, use a soft cloth to remove all rosin dust from the instrument and all parts of the bow except, of course, the hair itself.

2. When the instrument and bow are not in use, always keep them in the case.

3. Be certain that the latches on the case are always closed.

4. When the bow is not in use, loosen the hair until tension is removed from the arch of the stick. Three complete turns of the adjusting screw is usually sufficient. As a corollary to this principle, avoid excessive tension in the stick when tightening the bow. It should never be so tight that the arch is removed.

5. The bridge should be tilted slightly back toward the tailpiece.

6. String adjustors should not be turned all the way down so that they scratch the top of the instrument.

Avoiding the abuse of string instruments

7. Do not permit students to stuff music into their instrument cases.

8. If pegs are slipping, they may be treated with a commercial "peg dope." This is only a temporary solution, however, and the pegs should be eventually replaced or refitted.

9. Worn gears on string basses, adjustment screws on tuners, and adjustment screws on cello or bass end pins may all be lubricated with vaseline sparingly.

10. Improperly fitted pegs should be adjusted only by a competent repairman or shop.

The bridge is kept in position by the pressure of the strings. Under *no* circumstances should it be glued to the top. (In fact, nothing should be glued except by an expert.) The *high* side of the bridge is under the following strings for the various instruments: G string on the violin, C string on the viola, C string on the cello, and E string on the string bass.

A great deal of unnecessary repair work results from improper storage. Keep instruments out of excessively dry areas or damp basements and away from radiators and hot-air registers. The ideal temperature is about 60 degrees Fahrenheit with a relative humidity of about 45–50%. Loosen the strings when storing for an extended period of time.

Be careful that storage facilities are constructed in such a manner that the instruments cannot fall or bump each other. The cost of proper construction for storage is a saving well worth the investment.

> Competency 3:   Be able to identify the essentials for proper adjustment of string instruments.

Purchasing String Equipment

When selecting string instruments for school or private use, the manner of construction and the materials used, as described in the preceding sections, should be carefully noted. "Playability" of string instruments is so dependent on proper construction and correct adjustment and alignment that it is recommended that instruments conform to these standards regardless of the price bracket in which they may fall. The selection of instruments should not be based solely on a low initial price. Often inferior instruments eventually cost more than better ones in terms of repairs and loss of instruction time. The table on page 26 lists standard and junior sizes of string instruments.

A few comments on specifications are in order.

How to examine an instrument for purchase

1. All string instruments should be hand made and individually planed, sandpapered, adjusted, and tested.

2. Instruments should be made of matched woods that have been seasoned for a minimum of seven years.

3. Construction:

   a. All joints should be glued tightly and reinforced with four full corner blocks and solid upper and lower blocks and with full lining inside of top and back.

   b. All edges should be glued securely.

   c. Cracks, if any, should be properly repaired (reinforced and glued).

   d. Inlaid purfling is preferred.

   e. The bass bar should be of harder spruce than wood used for the top itself. The bass bar must be glued in and not carved out from top wood.

4. Trimmings:

   a. Pegs—ebony or rosewood. "Nonslip" pegs, such as those made by Caspari or DeJacques are recommended.

   b. Fingerboard—ebony. For basses and cellos, it may be of rosewood treated to resist absorption.

   c. Nut and saddle—ebony.

   d. Tailpiece—ebony.

5. Attachments:

   a. Chin rests—ebony, plastic, or rosewood.

   b. Strings—good quality, properly matched.

      E (violin): stainless steel with adjuster
      A (violin, viola, violoncello): gut or aluminum wound on gut
      D (all instruments): aluminum wound on gut
      G (all instruments): silver wound on gut
      C (viola, cello): silver wound on gut

String-bass strings are primarily made of steel. Steel strings always should be provided with adjusters (violin, viola, cello).

Proper Adjustment

One of the hidden costs in the procurement and maintenance of string instruments is the expense involved in proper adjustment. One cannot place enough emphasis on this item. It is of utmost importance since it affects intonation, tone quality, ease of playing, and basic instruction. A less expensive instrument that is properly adjusted is far more valuable for a student's development than a fine, expensive instrument improperly adjusted.

Imported instruments are packed in cases, shipped across oceans, and stored for extended periods of time to await delivery. The extreme humidity encountered during the voyage and the sharp climatic changes will cause changes in wooden parts of the instruments. This problem alone contributes much to maladjustment of string equipment.

Some of the items to examine for proper adjustment are the following:

1. *Peg alignment.* Pegs should be properly fitted so that they are snug at both sides of the peg box. In addition, they should be aligned in such a way that there is adequate clearance for each string above the peg in front of it. Under no circumstances should the end of the string be in a position where it can be forced into the peg-box wall.

2. *Fingerboard.* The fingerboard should be slightly concave without any warpage. When warped or worn, it interferes with intonation and causes a buzzing sound. A ruler placed on edge on top of the fingerboard will indicate if there is any warping.

3. *Fingerboard nut.* The nut should be checked carefully to see that it is not too low and that the spacing of the string grooves is correct so that the strings may enter the peg box and be wound properly.

4. *Bridge.* The entire surface of each foot of the bridge should be in contact with the top of the instrument. The height must be correct so that it does not require excessive finger pressure to play. If it is too low, it will interfere with the tone and hinder proper finger placement. The grooves should be deep enough to hold each string in place.

5. *Tailpiece.* The end of the tailpiece should come even with the center of the saddle but not extend beyond it. Under no circumstances should the tailpiece touch the body of the instrument or any of its components (chin rest, etc.).

6. *End pin.* On the cello and the bass be certain that the end pin slides freely can be easily adjusted to the height of the player.

7. *Sound post.* The sound post is located immediately behind the right foot of the bridge. The distance between the back of the bridge and the front of the post is approximately one-half of the thickness of the post.

8. *Bow.* The bow wire should be silver and soldered at each end. The bow screen should turn freely and the frog should be seated securely so that it does not wobble. Check to see that the hair tightens evenly to a desirable amount of tension and, conversely, that it may be properly but not excessively relaxed when the frog is in full forward position. Tighten the stick about two or three turns and sight down it to be certain that it is straight.

9. *Bow Hair.* For a variety of reasons, such as oil from contact with the skin, dust, or just rubbing, the hair on the bow may fail to hold rosin. When a player senses that the hair is not gripping the strings, he should replace it. This may be necessary even while the bow still has its full knot of hair.

10. *Strings.* Ideally, strings are matched for perfect fifths. When a string becomes false, it is virtually impossible to tune and the tone is affected. False strings should be replaced. (Do not wait until they break.) Long before an E string goes false, it becomes "dead." Although it still may be reasonably true in pitch, it no longer has the clear, ringing brilliance it had, especially in the high register. The violin E should be changed frequently. (The single most dramatic thing that can be done to improve the sound of the school's violin section is to have all the violinists change their E strings one week before a concert or contest.)

11. *Putting a string on an instrument.* After selecting the appropriate string, insert the end of the string through the hole in the peg. Pull it through sufficiently so that you can loop the end *under* the body of the string or at least one full turn of the peg. (See Figure 2–1.)

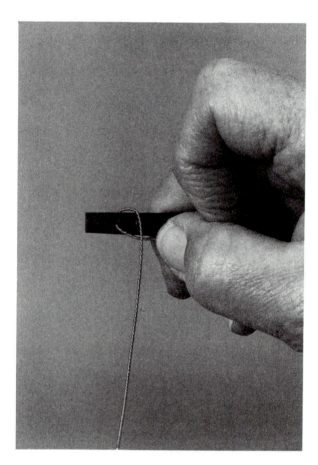

Figure 2–1   Inserting the string. (Courtesy IU Photographic Services)

It is useful to have a pair of tweezers to pull the string after it has been inserted and fed through the peg hole.

After completing the initial step, wind the string straight so that the body of the string moves evenly toward the head of the peg. This is extremely important: it assures that strings do not cross each other in the box. If this occurs, pressure from one string will affect the pitch of the other strings. In addition, improper winding makes the peg extremely difficult to turn and hold. (See Figure 2–2a.)

Incorrect

Correct

Figure 2–2a   Incorrect and correct ways of winding
the string.

Figure 2–2b   Strings properly wound on all pegs

When using a metal string, loop it on the tuner and follow the first step. If it is a gut-core string, put the knotted end through the tail-piece hole and pull the string to the proper peg in the box and follow the first step. Be certain that the tied end of the string is pulled forward in the tail-piece slot.

Figure 2–3   Tuner and tone filter. (Courtesy IU Photographic Services)

Figure 2–4   Gut string with the knot pulled forward in the slot.

Activities and Check List

1. If this course is taught in a class, exchange instruments and examine each one to evaluate its care and maintenance.
2. Recommend needed repairs and replacement parts for the instruments examined.

Selecting an Instrument of Proper Size

It is essential that students be given instruments in direct proportion to their growth. Nothing is more discouraging to the beginner than to be forced to play on an instrument that is too small or too large for his or her physical stature (see Figure 2–5). Because physical stature varies dramati-

Fitting the instrument to the child

Incorrect (too large)

Figure 2–5

cally within each age group, it is difficult to set up a uniform structure for selecting the size of an instrument. Each individual must be measured in accordance with his or her physical development (see Fig. 2–6).

Correct

Figure 2–6

Violin and viola. Extend the student's left arm palm up, and select the size instrument that enables him or her to curl fingers around the scroll and into the peg box comfortably.

Cello. Holding the instrument with the knees, at the bouts, should allow the student to have a correct left-hand position. If the position is correct, the student should be able to play a minor third between the first and fourth finger without distorting the fingers (see pp. 52 and 93).

Double bass. The height of the instrument should be so that the nut is approximately level with the student's eyes and he or she should be able to play a major second comfortably between the first and fourth fingers (see pp. 55 and 94). In addition, the size should also be determined by the length of the student's bow arm when the bow is placed at the middle of the D string. The shoulders should remain fairly horizontal.

Activities and Check List

1. Examine your instrument and bow and see if they comply with the adjustments you identified.
2. Exchange instruments and bows with others in the class and check their equipment for adjustment.
3. Make a list of necessary adjustments to any parts of the instruments and bows listed above, and submit it to the shop for correction.

String Accessories

CASES

All string instruments should come with a case. Violin and viola cases for students are usually shaped to conform to the body of the instrument. They are either made of plywood covered with textured black vinyl or a molded plastic veneer. In addition, they should have two rings on the handle side of the case on which a carrying strap may be snapped. More expensive violin and viola cases are usually oblong shaped and are made with three-ply wood or a plastic substance, such as fiberglass.

Bags for cellos and double-basses may be made of nylon or cordura. Better bags are fleece lined, but all bags should have some type of lining to protect the instrument. A bag must have a sleeve for the bow and a compartment to accommodate rosin, strings, and other small accessories. More expensive cello and bass cases used mainly by professionals are made of three-ply plywood or a plastic compound. The interiors are blocked to protect the instrument and are covered with a plush, velour lining. Adjustable Velcro restraints secure the instrument in its case. In addition, double-bass and cello performers often use a trunk-type case for travel or shipping.

CHIN RESTS (see pages 3 and 8)

Lightweight chin rests for violin and viola are available in matte finish, plastic, or carved ebony. More expensive chin rests may be made of rosewood, boxwood, and better ebony. They all come in a variety of sizes and shapes to accommodate the differences that exist in individual neck and chin sizes (See Figure 2–7). Another concern that helps to determine which

Figure 2–7 (Used by permission of the Glaesel Stringed Instrument Division of the Selmer Co., Inc.)

shape is selected is comfort. Fitting the appropriate size and height of the chin rest to a student's physical make-up is essential for balance and ease of playing, especially as it is used to hold the instrument firmly between his or her chin or jaw and collar bone. A proper chin rest can contribute greatly toward the ease of playing; it should be comfortable and provide a sense of security for the student. A poorly fitted chin rest is not only uncomfortable, but it can cause calluses, swelling, and even damage to the jaw tissue. Individuals with sensitive skin may put a soft cloth or thin chamois over the chin rest. Commercial pads are also available to make the player more comfortable (e.g., *Strad Pad*).

Teachers should have a chin-rest key in their kits to assist students when the instrument is placed against their necks.

SHOULDER PADS

There is still controversy about the use of shoulder pads. There is agreement, however, that if a pad helps reduce tension between the left shoulder and the chin or jaw, it is desirable. Furthermore, a shoulder pad may help to prevent the player from raising the left shoulder against the body of the instrument.

There are numerous types of shoulder pads available. The choice will vary according to its comfort and contribution to the ease in playing. Many professionals merely fold a handkerchief or their coat lapel under the instrument. For young students, a sponge, secured with a rubber band to the violin or viola, is sufficient. Cushioned shoulder pads are undesirable, however, since their contact with the back of the instrument affects the tone (see figure 2–8).

A few of the types of shoulder pads are:

1. *Resonance*—The pad area is cushioned and covered with velvet to provide a secure contact surface. The feet are adjustable and covered with surgical tubing to protect the finish of the instrument.

2. *Willy Wolf Forte Primo and Secundo*—It is molded to fit the shape of the shoulder and both sides can be adjusted for height. The *Primo* is straight with concave sides while the *Secundo* is kidney shaped.

Figure 2–8 (Used by permission of the Glaesel Stringed Instrument Division of the Selmer Co., Inc.)

3. *Kinder Chinder*—This pad was developed especially for Suzuki violin students. The corduroy-covered foam pads cushion and give support to even the smallest Suzuki instrument. It is adjustable and attaches to the chin rest and the opposite bout.

4. *Playonair*—This consists of an inflatable pad with air pressure controlling the height. It comes in several shapes and sizes, and all fit violins and violas.

5. *Strad pad*—It is not a shoulder pad, but rather a covering that fits over the chin rest. It is ultra-soft and nonallergenic and helps to alleviate perspiration, pressure, and rubbing that cause discoloration on the necks of many violinists and violists.

ROSIN

All string instruments should come equipped with a cake of rosin. It enables the bow hair to get a better "grip" on the string, setting it into vibration. Without rosin, the bow hair slides on the string and restricts player from producing an appropriate tone.

The shapes of rosin cakes are either oblong, and come in box holders made of cork or wood, or round, mounted on cloth holders. The oblong cake is preferable for beginners because if it is dropped, it does not shatter as much as round cakes do.*

Virtually every string company has its brand of rosin. The choice depends on the individual's preference when experimenting with a variety of texture. Most important is that rosin for the violin and viola should not be used for the cello or string bass. Each has its own texture. Cello rosin is coarser and softer than violin/viola rosin and string bass rosin is coarser

---

* When applying rosin, hold the cake in the left hand and, with the right hand, rest the bow on top of the cake. The first finger of the right hand should rest on top of the stick while the remaining fingers hold the frog. The bow is then drawn several times back and forth with even pressure from the frog to the tip and back again.

and has a gummy consistency that is effective for the bass bow. Good rosin should stick excessively to the string. It should not leave excessive residue or dust on the instrument.

TUNERS

Tumers should always be used with metal-core strings. Because metal strings respond in pitch to the slightest adjustment, tuners are necessary to assist in this procedure. They can be immeasurable value in just the time conserved when tuning. They should *not* be used with gut strings.

To prevent buzzing noise, a tone filter is placed between the string and the bridge when using metal strings. In addition, these filters help prevent the metal string from cutting into the bridge. Filters usually are a piece of rubber or plastic shaped like a doughnut (See figure 2–3).

MUTES

The mute, which is attached to the top of the bridge, affects the tone color by reducing the amplitude of the vibrations of the bridge. This produces a softer, or *sotto voce,* tone. Like chin rests, there is a wide variety of mutes. Selection should be based on ease of use and the desired effect that one seeks.

Some representative styles of mutes are:

1. *Sihon:* A slide-on mute mounted on the strings, behind the bridge, the Sihon slides over the top of the bridge when needed. Permanently in place, it has the advantage of not being misplaced or lost.
2. *Tourte:* Advantageously mounted on the strings, between the tailpiece and the bridge, Tourte mutes are moved forward when needed.
3. *Wood:* Traditional mutes are usually made of ebony or pear wood and have two or three prongs (four in the case of cello or bass mutes) that clip on the bridge when needed.
4. *Heifetz:* A compromise between the traditional mute and the slide-on style, the Heifetz mute is made of rubber and mounted on the E string.

STRINGS

There are two types of strings: metal (steel) strings and gut-core strings. Because steel strings maintain their pitch better than gut-core strings, they present a distinct advantage to young players. In addition, steel strings require metal tuners, which make it easier to adjust pitch and save time in tuning. Furthermore, steel strings last longer than gut strings and produce a brighter, louder tone with less effort.

As students progress and are able to do their own tuning, they may switch to gut-core strings, which produce, in most cases, a better sound. The exception is the E string, which is a single strand of steel. (Many years ago even the E string was made of gut, but it lacked the brilliancy of the modern steel E.) In the final analysis the choice of string used depends on the individual's preference.

Some of the widely used brands are *Glaesel Chromium Steel, Dr. Thomastik Steel, Pirastro, Eudoxa, Wondertone, Black Label, Gold Label, Ancore,* among others. It is recommended that matched sets of strings be purchases when equipping instruments or replacing broken strings.

PART II

Developing String Programs in Schools

Developing String Programs in Schools

Creating Interest in Strings: Recruiting

A major responsibility of the string teacher is the task of bringing the joy of music making, and especially the thrill of playing a string instrument, to young people. Unfortunately, some teachers of strings approach this matter in the spirit of inducing pupils to take up the study of a string instrument principally for the purpose of building a school orchestra. The only valid purpose in creating interest in playing a string instrument should be, first of all, the musical growth and the musical pleasure of the pupils. If this is the genuine goal of the string program, there will be an orchestra—and a good one.

There are numerous ways of recruiting string players. Some of the most prevalent methods are described below and appraised from both positive and negative viewpoints.

The announcement method. This consists of making announcements, both in classrooms and in assemblies, with the hope that pupils may join the string program. Classroom teachers are asked to "talk it up." Parents are usually notified by mail, or else a printed announcement is sent home with pupils. For creating interest in strings, this is probably the *least* effective and the least dependable means.

The lecture method. A typical example of this approach is for the teacher to appear before the students with a violin or a set of string instruments. He tells something of the history of the instruments; how they are constructed; the materials of which they are made, etc. The demonstration is usually concluded with an explanation of the personal rewards of playing an instrument, and other such benefits. Pupils may find this demonstration "interesting," but as an agency for recruitment, it is usually not as effective as some other methods.

Attracting students to play string instruments

The guest artist performer. In an effort to arouse interest in playing a string instrument, some teachers who play well might perform before a class or student assembly, with the hope that students will be inspired to join the string program. Teachers who do not play so well themselves often bring in an outstanding performer for this purpose. This type of approach usually provides musical "entertainment" of a high order, but normally it induces only a few students to take up the study of string instruments. Perhaps the reason for this is the fact that even young people realize that to perform at such a high level of artistry requires unusual talent, plus many years of study and practice. Human beings are more inclined to want for themselves the things that they can accomplish and enjoy in a relatively short time.

The testing program. Many schools rely on a testing program. The tests are not intended to eliminate students but to offer a means of communicating with the students and their parents. Once the tests are completed, letters are sent home requesting a conference or inviting parents to a demonstration concert or meeting. The letters usually state the purpose and objectives of the school music program and how strings contribute to it; they may contain information on how the child will benefit from playing. Although the testing plan has met with some success, it can be misleading in that it may misrepresent the student's talent. Tests containing little or no data on reliability and validity have limited value.

The string performance unit.   A more desirable plan is to present a unit on instruments of the orchestra to the third- or fourth-grade music class. After a brief introductory period, students have the opportunity to actually experiment with each kind of string instrument. Those students who show interest are considered as potential string students. The plan has met with some success where sufficient time and/or money is allotted to the general music program; however, that is rarely the case.

The student string ensemble.   One of the more prevalent approaches used to create interest in strings is to select a group of students from the existing string program in the school, or from another school, and have them play for the music class. If this approach is used, it is a good idea to choose student performers whose ages approach the ages of the student audience. However, it is even better to have two performing groups: one group that is experienced and somewhat advanced, and a second group that has had only a year or so of experience. The idea is that students in the audience are likely to feel that they, too, can do this.

The participation method.   This is by far the most effective means of creating interest in playing a string instrument. The children are given a quick, five-minute lesson on finding the open strings, and then they actually play the instruments while the orchestra or piano plays melody and accompaniment. The children experience playing, and they love it.

The hands-on approach   There is no substitute for personal participation in an activity. This is true in all life situations. For example, boys and girls might enjoy watching other boys and girls play some sport, but only in a passive or semipassive way. The real thrill comes from the experience of trying it oneself—even if one's efforts do not conform to all of the niceties of refined techniques. To become personally involved in something, whether or not by design, is to come closer to it. In using the participation method, the author has observed many occasions where people—both young and old—who thought they had a strong dislike for music suddenly experienced an entirely different attitude; they actually wanted to become active music makers. It is human nature to want to work hardest at the things that have personal value and satisfaction, that instill an inner feeling of success, or at least suggest that success is attainable, even if it requires effort on the part of the individual.

The short piece that follows is a good example of music that can be used in the participation method.

In the final analysis, the most effective agent for the promotion of string playing is the music teacher. It is the teacher's genuine enthusiasm and belief in the inherent value of his or her task that sustains the interest of the students. Good teachers maintain a kindly attitude toward their class. While they must insist on a high standard of performance, teachers should never be unkind or destructive. Students thrive on praise and recognition, and teachers should be generous with these if interest is to be maintained.

Flow Gently Sweet Afton

Arranged by Ernest E. Harris

The Developmental String Program

String study programs should offer a well-organized, sequential series of experiences that promote interest and contribute toward the development of the individual player. They should give students a musical objective for increasing and refining their technical proficiency so that as their "performance ability" improves, so does their musical understanding and sensitivity.

Students should be made aware of study objectives from their earliest stages of instruction. These goals may be in terms of physical movement, performance, skill (bowing, etc.), or specific pieces of music in their repertoire. As they achieve these goals, they enjoy an awareness of their own progress and success. A useful technique to motivate pupils is to make special assignments to individuals as well as class assignments. A performance, whether in front of a class, a homeroom, or a parent's meeting, is always a good incentive to practice. It is also helpful to keep daily practice records. If checked conscientiously, they provide another form of commitment toward developing the skills required for successful string playing.

Concerts and public performances are almost always motivating. These may be unison solos, including pieces for students from every level of proficiency, or informal demonstrations. Ensemble playing, introduced in the early stages of instruction, should be nurtured and encouraged until it reaches the sophisticated level of actual chamber-music performance.

SELECTING STUDENTS

In many schools the theory prevails that "only the best and most talented students should be selected for string players." This theory has worked to the detriment of school orchestras. It conveys the idea that strings exist on a unique plateau and only the elite should be chosen to play them.

It is only natural that teachers prefer to work with students who are relatively far along in their musical growth. There are, however, many examples of students who indicated little ability when "tested," but who developed at a rapid rate after being exposed to musical experiences.

Flexibility in the selection process

Schools should provide a trial period that would let any child who exhibits genuine interest have an opportunity to experiment with several string instruments. Thus, over a period of several months, a teacher could observe the child's musical growth, his musical awareness, and the development of his auditory perception. Additional information could be obtained from the classroom teacher, who observes the child's musical behavior pattern daily.

Physical characteristics.   Strings are the one instrumental family in the orchestra that is completely adaptable in size to accommodate the physical growth and characteristics of each child. No other family of instruments provides such flexibility. To assure maximum success, this advantage should be utilized to its utmost. Even the preschool child has a choice of instruments down to a one-sixteenth-size violin.

Physical characteristics in a student's choice of a string instrument

When selecting string players, it is well to observe the spread and general flexibility of the palm and fingers of the left hand, the size of the fingers, and the arm length. Children with short, stubby fingers, or those with extremely slender fingers will have some difficulty. But it is not necessary to be unduly concerned about the little finger. With sufficient spread of the palm and proper use of the left elbow, a small fourth finger is not a serious handicap. Children with a larger palm spread and wider fingers may choose correspondingly larger instruments; however, for the most auspicious beginning, the students should have exhibited some interest in these larger instruments. Much will depend on the teacher's judicious guidance.

Measuring a student for size.   Many methods are employed to measure a student for the correct size of instrument (see pp. 13–14). For the violin or viola, another procedure is suggested: Measure the student's left arm from his armpit to the tip of his middle finger; then use the chart given below:

Arm Length	Violin	Viola
Under 18 in.	One-quarter size or smaller	—
18–21 in.	Half size	—
21–24 in.	Three-quarter size	Junior
24 in. or over	Full size	Three-quarter size

The cello and bass size is determined by a combination of factors—the student's arm length and his height. The following chart gives a rough guide for proper size.

Arm Length	Height	Cello	Bass
Under 18 in.	50 in.	One-quarter size or smaller	—
18–22 in.	52 in.	Half size	—
20–22 in.	56 in.	Three-quarter size	Half size
22–24 in.	60 in.	Full size	Three-quarter size (This is a full size for school use.)

Visual guidelines

There are some visual guidelines. For the cello, the instrument is too large if the student has to drop his right shoulder and body to play at the tip of the bow. When he is seated properly, the top part of the lower bouts should be about at knee height. The neck block should come up to the student's breastbone.

For the bass, the student should also be able to play at the tip of the bow without dropping his right shoulder, and the fingerboard nut should be about even with the student's left eye. The length of the end pin can be adjusted to the player's height. The left hand should be able to encompass a major second (one full tone on the scale) with the first to the fourth fingers on the strings.

When in doubt, it is better to recommend a smaller instrument rather than one that is too large.

Measuring the bow length

It is not uncommon to find that an instrument selected according to the size of the left hand may utilize a bow that is too long for the student's right hand. In this case, have the student hold the stick at the frog as though he or she were going to play, and then tip it so that it is parallel to the right arm. Mark the stick with a piece of tape at the point where it reaches the student's shoulder; this indicates the length of his or her full bow. To have the student play beyond this point would necessitate swinging the arm away from proper bowing paths and would result in poor habits. It is not necessary to get a different bow, although it is preferable. As the student grows, the point of his or her full bow will be extended until it reaches the full length of the stick. It is important that the student should not try to play beyond the marked point until able to do so.

Measurements and Terminology of Sizes

I.   Instrument Terminology for Measurements

a. The body length is measured from the top shoulder (upper edge, where the neck joins the body) to the end of the lower bout (base of the instrument).

b. The string length is measured from the edge of the nut (where fingerboard meets nut) to the bridge. Actually, it is the open-string length that vibrates when played.

1. Violin and Viola: The body distance (diapason) between the inside notch of the F-hole (on the soundpost side) to the upper edge of the top (where the neck joins the body) should represent three-fifths of the string length.

2. Cello: The diapason should represent ten-seventeenths of the string length.

3. Bass: The diapason should represent four-sevenths of the string length.

II.   Instrument Measurements

Violin	Size	Body Length		String Length	
		Inches	cm	Inches	cm
Standard (full)	4/4	14	35.56	12 7/8	32.70
Intermediate	3/4	13 1/4	33.66	12	30.50
Junior	1/2	12 7/16	31.59	11 5/16	28.73
Bantam	1/4	11	27.94	10 1/64	26.44
Bantam	1/8	10	25.40	9 5/32	23.26
Bantam	1/10	9 1/4	23.50	8 9/32	21.03
Bantam	1/16	8 1/2	21.59	7 25/64	18.80

Bantam sizes vary, depending upon the country of manufacture.

Viola	Size	Inches	cm	Inches	cm
Standard (full)	Large	16 1/2 and up	41.90 and up	15	38.1
Standard (full)		16	40.64	15	38.1
Standard (full)		15 1/2	39.40	14 11/64	36.0
Standard (full)	Small	15	38.1	13 31/32	35.5
Intermediate		14	35.56	12 7/8	32.70
Junior		13 1/4	33.66	12	30.50

Cello	Size	Inches	cm	Inches	cm
Standard (full)	4/4	29 5/8	75.25	27 1/2	69.9
Intermediate	3/4	27 5/16	69.40	24 3/4	62.87
Junior	1/2	25 1/2	64.77	23 1/4	59.05
Bantam	1/4	22 3/4	57.79	20 3/4	52.71
Bantam	1/8	20 1/8	51.12	18 18/32	47.15

Bass	Size	Inches	cm	Inches	cm
Standard	3/4	43 1/4 to	109.86 to	41 1/2 to	105.40 to
Standard	3/4	44 1/2	113.0	43 5/16	110.0
Intermediate	1/2	38 5/8 to	98.11 to	38 3/4 to	98.43
Intermediate	1/2	41 1/4	104.78	38 3/4	98.43
Junior	1/4	35	88.9	—	—
Bantam	1/8	—	—	—	—

III. Bows

a. The bow length is measured from the tip to the end of the screw button. Bows should be proportionate to the size of the instrument used.

Violin Bow	Size	Length	
		Inches	cm
Standard	4/4	29 1/4	74.30
Intermediate	3/4	27	68.58
Junior	1/2	24 1/2	62.23
Bantam	1/4	22 1/8	56.20
Bantam	1/8	19 1/4	48.90
Bantam	1/10*	19 1/4	48.90
Bantam	1/16*	16 3/16	42.70

*Both use same size fiberglass bow, 1/16 size

Viola Bow	Size	Length	
		Inches	cm
Standard	4/4*	29 1/4	74.30
Intermediate	3/4*	29 1/4	74.30
Junior	1/2*	27	68.60

*Intermediate (14") violas use the same length bow as a 4/4 violin, but the viola of 14" or larger should use a viola bow under all circumstances. Smaller violas may use violin bows.

Cello Bow	Size	Length	
		Inches	cm
Standard	4/4	28 1/8	71.40
Intermediate	3/4	26 7/16	67.15
Junior	1/2	25 1/2	64.77
Bantam	1/4	23 1/2	59.69
Bantam	1/8	20 5/8	52.39
Bantam	1/10	17 1/2	44.45

Bass Bow	Size	Length	
		Inches	cm
Standard	French 3/4	28 3/4	73.03
Standard	German 3/4	30 3/8	77.15
Intermediate	French 1/2	26 1/2	67.30
Intermediate	German 1/2	27 3/4	70.49
Junior	1/4-use half-size bows.		

French or German (Butler) bass bows are acceptable in all sizes

    b. Bow Materials
        1. Pernambuco wood—first choice for better quality instruments
        2. Brazilwood
        3. Fiberglass—acceptable for 1/16 and 1/8 size instruments
    c. Now Hair Materials
        1. Natural horse hair—unbleached hair
        2. Synthetic hair—must be texturized
        3. White hair is preferred for advanced (solo) students, however, mixed hair is quite acceptable.
        4. Bow hair should be "sighted down" to make sure there are no crossed or twisted hairs.

SELECTING MATERIALS

There is no one "method" book that will address all problems and automatically ensure success. A music teacher should carefully examine all the books available and select materials on the basis of his or her own basic approach to teaching strings. Nothing is more revealing of a teacher's attitude about strings and about music in general than the materials he or she selects. It is the teacher's choices that will determine, in a sense, the musical development of students.

In establishing criteria for selecting music books, a few pertinent questions may be used as guidelines: (1) Does the material contain sufficient music of quality to challenge the inherent musical needs of the children? (2) Is there a proper skill sequence to promote technical as well as musical growth? Does it contain scales, bowing studies, rhythmic studies, and interval exercises? (3) Does the material embody the essential, basic principles that affect technique? (4) Does it offer music attractive enough to sustain a student's interest and keep him or her working diligently? (5) Are there enough pictures to illustrate proper techniques? (6) Is the estimated rate of progress correct for the purpose? (7) If the music is to be performed in public, is it within the scope of the student's technical proficiency so that it may be prepared within a reasonable amount of rehearsal time? (8) Does the material or "method" promote proper attitudes toward music as an art form?

Criteria

Music selected for school string groups should be carefully edited and arranged so that it preserves the general effect desired by the composer.

In addition, students should not be subjected only to skill studies. From the beginning, every effort should be made to provide satisfying musical experiences. Enjoyment and perceivable progress are the essential ingredients for success. They should be the major considerations in the selection of all music.

MULTIPLE-PART MUSIC

The opportunity to perform still seems to be the major incentive for practice. Unfortunately, students are all too often forced to perform music that is beyond their technical and musical ability. This not only inhibits proper instruction but contributes to improper playing habits and false standards.

Such a mistake is entirely unnecessary. Through multiple-part music, students can still have thrilling, satisfying experiences without being forced into premature solo performances. A music director planning a group performance may simplify any part that is beyond the technical range of a student's ability without destroying the musical effect. In addition, there are many compositions specially written for this type of performance. One example is Vaughan Williams's *Concerto Grosso for String Orchestra,* which even includes parts for an open-string orchestra. (The criteria for such music should be that the easy parts should be within the technical limitations of the less skilled players and that the overall sound should be substantially satisfying to the more mature players.)

Flexibility in technical proficiency

The Oberlin, Ohio, community has in past years held an effective string festival; it always featured a multiple-part composition that included beginning string classes, the string players of the high-school and college orchestras, and string players in the adult community.

Karl Kroeger has composed for the Eugene, Oregon, school system a *Prelude for Massed String Orchestras,* which is now available through University Microfilms, Ann Arbor, Michigan. This composition employs beginning elementary, advanced elementary, junior-high-school, and high-school orchestras, offering valid motivation and encouragement for players of lesser ability. It also provides learning experiences that include living, practical examples of good tone quality, good posture, and proper performance habits. There is a tremendous potential in this type of music for the school orchestra.

Heterogeneous and Homogeneous String Classes

There is no real agreement on the merits of homogeneous versus heterogeneous string classes. In schools the choice is too often dictated by expediency and schedules.

A good formula might be that with the younger students (elementary), single-instrument classes are preferable. As students mature, they become more interested in the composite sound of the orchestra, and then the heterogeneous approach becomes the more favorable.

In secondary schools (junior and senior high schools), departmentalized schedules make it possible for a string class to meet daily. Here the students progress faster and are able to start playing simple ensemble music. In this situation the heterogeneous class provides greater flexibility, sustains interest, and offers a greater variety of literature and activities for instruction purposes.

On the other hand, the homogeneous class makes teaching easier. There is less concern with providing interesting activities for violin players, for example, while working on a specific problem involving bass players. In addition, among the various instruments there are several differences in hand position and technique that might be confusing if taught in a mixed class. (See "Common Errors," p. 66–72). In the final analysis, the teacher must study his own situation and determine what is best for his type of program.

Techniques for teaching string classes

In both heterogeneous and homogeneous classes there are certain techniques for class teaching that should be utilized. Among these are the following: (1) Do not remain static. Circulate among the class and work with individuals at all times. (2) Devise a variety of activities that enable the individual to perform and still involve the entire class. For example, an individual plays—the group responds; class fingers the notes while an individual performs; student plays—the class analyzes; recital hours, etc. (3) Utilize a variety of bowings even in "unison" performance, to allow for individual difference, (some pizzicato, others arco; some using slurred bowings, others marcato; etc.).

Elizabeth A. H. Green in her book, *Teaching Stringed Instruments In Classes,* published by the American String Teachers Association, lists the following ten general goals for a year's work (p. 32):[1]

"**1.** Getting the ear to hear pitch and to know which way to move a finger to play perfectly in tune. . . .

2. Keeping the fingers down on the strings as much as possible. . . .

3. Keeping the fingers close to the strings when they are in the air, off the strings. . . .

4. Building slurred bowing. . . .

5. Improving constantly the closeness of half steps. . . .

6. Acquiring some knowledge of and facility in on-octave scales.

7. Sometimes the vibrato motion is started. . . .

8. Memorizing various tunes which can be played as solos. . . .

9. Developing tone quality throughout the entire first year together with a proper use of whole-bow and half-bow strokes.

---

[1]Elizabeth A. H. Green. *Teaching Stringed Instruments in Classes.* ASTA/MENC Publications Sales, Reston, Virginia, 1987, p. 32.

10. Laying a foundation for future speed and clarity in the left-hand finger action. . . . "

Activities and Check List

1. Identify and discuss the advantages and disadvantages of the various methods of recruiting string students.
2. What are the physical characteristics that should assist one in selecting the string instrument he or she may play?
3. Discuss the advantages and disadvantages of heterogeneous and homogeneous class teaching.
4. What are some of the skills that students should develop during the first year of instruction?

The Second-Year String Class

The objectives of a second-year string class are (1) improving reading ability through ensemble experiences, (2) further developing the use of the bow arm, (3) introducing the use of positions, and (4) developing a vibrato. The challenge in a class situation is how to provide this instruction to individuals of varying abilities and still maintain full class activity throughout the period.

Combining individual instruction with class instruction

Since private study is the best solution for developing facility and tonal concepts on an instrument, and since the class supplies the best ensemble experience, it is best to combine some of the elements of the private studio with the socially motivating advantages of the classroom. Under these conditions, the materials used in a class would include études as well as ensemble music.

To implement this twofold plan, each student in a mixed-instrument class should have a separate étude book. Assignments are made to each group of players, and students then spend half of the period in supervised unison practice and half in ensemble playing.

Thus the director may spend a part of each daily period teaching a homogeneous group in the classroom while the remaining students are assigned practice rooms. Individual lessons need not be given during the instruction period, but members of the group should receive help as it is needed. Études may be played in unison and rehearsed as if they were unison sections in a composition while the teacher circulates around the room making individual corrections. Individuals may be asked to play certain significant passages, and, to keep everyone occupied, those who are not playing may finger the passage silently. The group may be asked to analyze an individual's performance. Some of the students may be asked to prepare études as solos and perform a short recital during the lesson period. Here again silent exercises may be utilized while an individual is playing.

Designating a variety of bowings will help to accommodate the differing rates of acquiring skills in a class. For example, one group may be reviewing an eighth-note étude with a détaché bowing, while another group that had performed the exercise satisfactorily the previous day plays the same étude with two slurs and two separate bows; that is

This manner of teaching not only provides for individual abilities, but begins to develop the second objective, which is expanded use of the bow arm.

Use of student aides

During the period of homogeneous instruction, be certain that an aide, who may be a class chairman or an advanced student, is constantly supervising the students in the practice rooms. When the proper attitude has been established, students enjoy practicing in groups and helping each other. One student can take charge of the group while the director checks the practice rooms to see that all is going well. Instruction should take only part of a period; the remainder should be spent checking and evaluating assignments. All of these conditions help impel students to work.

Ensemble playing. Facility in reading music is best developed through ensemble playing. There is a good deal of easy ensemble or string-orchestra music available. Many of the heterogeneous-class methods have a second book that can be used as an easy orchestra folio. During the ensemble-playing segment of the instruction period, students learn to play under the direction of a baton, and there should be considerable emphasis on dynamics, balance, phrasing, ensemble relationships, and similar elements of ensemble playing.

Private instruction. Playing in the school orchestra is a special activity designed for students with special interests and abilities. Therefore it is justifiable to encourage students who qualify to play in the orchestra to study privately, especially when interest and talent warrant it. In addition, as better string-class instruction is offered during the early years, more students are motivated to study privately as a result of their musical growth in the class.

However, in the public schools, circumstances do not always permit private lessons. There may be financial restrictions, or some students may live where teachers are not available. It then becomes incumbent upon the school music teacher to provide instruction for these children in class.

ELECTRONIC AIDS AND TECHNOLOGY

During the latter half of the twentieth century several computer types of equipment (hardware and software) were developed to assist string teachers with their teaching. For psychological reasons, some teachers may resist using this equipment, however, as some of these items facilitate learning, teachers should take advantage of them. Computer-Assisted Instruction (CAI) can enhance learning; learn to use it. Computers can assist with mundane tasks with considerable efficiency, and there is ample information on how and what to use of this equipment.

To assist the teacher in finding and selecting programs and equipment, some suggestions are offered. The list is limited and intended merely to introduce the prospective teacher to the CAI capabilities offered by computers for music instruction.

Name	Capability	Address
AMADEUS	A Digital Signal Analyzer, a MIDI (musical instrument digital interface) Converter and a Precision Tuner, It offers instruction on pitch, rhythm, tone quality and amplitude.	P.O. Box 639 Grapevine, TX 76099 Ph 1-800-222-7536
Vivace	Computer-based, it attaches to either a MacIntosh with a single cable or a PC Windows computer. It provides accompaniments to simple solo pieces and progresses through concerti. The literature also includes a wide variety of jazz styles for the student's enjoyment. Although most of the accompaniments are for wind players, string accompaniments are being added.	Coda Music Technology 6210 Bury Dr. Eden Prairie, MN 55346-1718 1-800-843-2066, Ext. 7
Video Camera with playback capabilities	There is no more effective teaching tool than a video camera, for it enables a student to examine and assess his or her playing position. Through the use of the camera, students may actually see themselves playing. The camera may be adjusted to focus at various angles so that if there is a specific problem, whether in the bow arm or in holding the instrument, students can see themselves and receive immediate feedback.	A variety of sources
TAPMASTER	TAP is a comprehensive program that develops music-reading skills and rhythmic ability. It consists of cassette tapes and accompanying books, stereo headphones, and an optional acrylic stand.	Temporal Acuity Products, Inc. Bldg. 1, Suite 200 300-120th Ave. N.E. Bellvue, WA 98005
Teaching Music with Technology	A guide to using technology in teaching music, this book helps clarify the vast technological changes taking place in education today.	Advanced Technologies 1988 State Line Rd. South Bend, IN 46637
MIDI-SCHOOL	It features an 8-track sequencer, glossary with auto-index, interactive lessons to enhance retention, and a built-in lesson planner.	Advanced Technologies 1988 State Line Rd. South Bend, IN 46637
Electronic Instruments		Advanced Technologies 1988 State Line Rd. South Bend, IN 46637
a. Strados Violin	The Strados from Zeta Music Systems is *not MIDI compatible.* It does give the violinist the ability to produce the sound of an acoustic violin at a volume necessary for the stage.	
b. Classic Violin	MIDI compatible, the "Classic" maintains the playing surface and dimensions of the traditional violin. A volume wheel is located on the side of the violin that allows the bow band to adjust the volume without releasing the bow.	
c. Jazz Violin	Responsive to all playing styles, the Zeta Jazz Violin, because of its ergonomic shape, facilitates reaching to all positions and increases playing speed.	
Zeta "Uprite" Bass	It is a solid-body electric double bass that captures the feel and tone of a traditional upright. Zeta's bridge transducer system utilizes four separate preamps and one pair of pickups per string.	Advanced Technologies 1988 State Line Rd. South Bend, IN 46637

Name	Capability	Address
Zeta Viola	Similar to the Jazz Violin model but adjusted to viola specifications.	
Zeta Cello	It provides the feel found in traditional instruments. The two pickups and separate preamplifiers for each string allow a clear distinct cello tone at any volume.	
Pepper National Music Network (PNMN)	The network allows the music teacher using a computer, modem and phone lines to participate in forums, send and receive electronic mail, contact industry companies and organizations, research repertoire, communicate with MENC and state organizations, as well as upload and download music computer files.	1-800-345-6296
ASTA Media Resource Center	Contains films and instruction materials that cover all aspects of string playing.	ASTA Media Resource Center Robert Gillespie, Director 110 Weigel Hall 1866 College Road The Ohio State University Columbus, OH 43210-1170
Pitch Master	The Pitch Master System is a comprehensive program that teaches basic pitch concepts and sight-reading skills in a performance context.	Temporal Acuity Products, Inc. Bldg. 1, Suite 200 300-120th Ave. N.E. Bellevue, WA 98005
Band in a Box Version 6.0	Available for IBM, Macintosh, and Atari computers, it can be used to recognize and verbalize rhythmic patterns. It may also be used to generate practice tapes that motivate students to practice at home. Students are encouraged to improvise using the instrument.	P.G. Music Inc. 266 Elmwood Ave. Suite 1100 Buffalo, NY 14222
The Art of Sequencing by Don Muro	A textbook (also available as a video) on the technique of sequencing, this primer gives the reader (viewer) a clearer understanding of the sequencer, MIDI, and the process of sequencing.	CPP/Belwin, Inc. 15800 N.W. 48th Ave. Miami, Florida, 33014

The Strados SV-245

The Zeta jazz MIDI violin JV-205   The Zeta ZB-224 upright bass

(Photos used by permission of the ZETA Music Company.)

Additional Resources for Technology

Association for Technology in Music
    Instruction (ATMI)
School of Music
University of Massachusetts/Amherst
Amherst, MA 01003

Educational Resources
1550 Executive Dr.
Elgin, IL 60123

Electronic Courseware Systems, Inc.
1210 Lancaster Dr.
Champaign, IL 61821

CD-ROM Warehouse
1720 Oak St.
Lakewood, NJ 08701

Educorp
7434 Trade St.
San Diego, CA 92121-2410

Sweetwater Sounds, Inc.
5335 Bass Rd.
Fort Wayne, IN 46808

Strolling Strings

A newly developed program designed to attract students with the same appeal offered by the swing choir, the stage band, and the marching band is the strolling-strings ensemble. Although to some this may appear to be a recent phenomenon, professional string players have been strolling performers in clubs, restaurants and at special events for many, many years. What is new is the utilization of strolling in an educational setting to promote educational values.

Like the other "pop" organizations, Strolling Strings is "show biz" and serves as an excellent recruiting medium. However, beyond the popular appeal, there are musical, educational, and technical benefits that participants derive from this activity. To stroll, students must memorize their music. This enables them to concentrate on bowing, musical phrasing and improved intonation. Each student is a soloist; it is a one-on-one activity. It helps them to develop confidence by being in close contact with their audience; there are no "last chair" players.

Music written especially for this group is arranged in a light, popular style and designed to have audience appeal.

James "Red" McLeod has arranged four complete shows for strolling-string groups:

A Music Buffet of All-Time Favorites
A Night at the Symphony
A Night in Vienna
Strolling Around the World

In addition to those listed above, there are available six "show-stoppers":

The Grand Stroll, arr. McLeod
The Grand Stroll II, arr. McLeod
Holiday Salute, arr. McLeod
The Monte Csardas, Monti/McLeod
Salute to Freedom, arr. McLeod
Themes from *The Nutcracker*, Tchaikovksy/McLeod arr.

All of the music listed is published by the Neil A. Kjos Music Company, 4380 Jutland Drive, San Diego, California, 92117-0894. A tape that describes the program, *Strolling Strings*, is also available upon request from Kjos or from the ASTA Media Center at The Ohio State University, School of Music, Columbus, Ohio.

MENC has published as a part of its Getting Started series, *Getting Started with Strolling Strings,* compiled by Robert Gillespie.

Twentieth-Century Schools of String Teaching

SUZUKI APPROACH

In 1964, at a meeting of the Music Educators' National Conference in Philadelphia, Shinichi Suzuki presented concepts regarding the musical education of preschool children in Japan that might well be called revolutionary. One of Suzuki's basic ideas was that educators had been underestimating the learning potential of small children. He also contended that environmental factors are far more important in the musical growth of a child than is so-called talent. Though the users of the present book may not be directly involved in preschool instruction, all teachers of string instruments should be informed and prepared to discuss the Suzuki method when they become involved in school music programs.

Preschool instruction

Shinichi Suzuki

Dr. Suzuki's use of the word *environment* did not refer to a socioeconomic setting. What he suggested was a conditioning program based on a planned and supervised program of musical training at an early age. He proposed that any teacher can provide a stimulating musical environment based on an ear-conditioning program that utilizes musical examples that have proved to be motivating for children. On this premise, any child can play the violin just as he learns to speak his native tongue. Incidentally, this does not disregard the talent factor: the ultimate level that the child will achieve is determined by this factor.

Objectives

Dr. Suzuki has pointed out that a child learns to speak his native or "mother" tongue through the natural method of imitating his mother and other members of the family, not by formal reading materials. By applying this principle to violin playing, he has proved that much of what we have assumed to be "inborn genius" actually has been developed by applying proper educational principles at an early age. Basic to his method is listening to high-quality performances on a recording or tape. It is his contention that music should be learned from listening before music reading. Each piece is memorized from listening to the tape or record for every lesson.

Another fundamental principle in this approach is the absolute mastery of each step before proceeding to the next. One should not measure progress by quantity or speed but rather by quality. The Suzuki method concentrates on fostering proper bowing, the production of a "beautiful" tone, the proper playing position and posture, and good intonation.

A significant feature of this program is the inclusion of interested parents and, as always, sensitive, enthusiastic, patient teachers. Through parental involvement, playing an instrument becomes a family affair—a joint exploration into the joys of making music. In addition, by attending the lesson the parent becomes more responsible for providing the necessary home environment and overseeing the practice period.

Lessons in the pure Suzuki schools are private although other students and parents are in attendance so that even a private lesson has an audience. Periodically, teachers will bring their students together at recitals, concerts, or conferences for "play-ins" where solo literature is performed *en masse*. These programs are designed not only as an opportunity to culminate certain learning eperiences at various levels, but also to inform parents and friends about the progress the children are making. A fundamental premise in the Suzuki philosophy is that a child should not discard a composition once it is learned. It is only then that musical, artistic learning really asserts itself. By frequent repetition the child refines each piece. Review, reinforcement, and "play-ins" provide enjoyable experiences and motivate students to retain pieces they have learned.

In summary, the Suzuki approach is based on the following:

1. An organized sequence of musical materials that follow an order based on technical, musical levels of ability,

2. Recordings by leading artists that provide models for students to emulate,

3. Parents' attendance at every lesson so that they may assist in the learning process,

4. Games that use physical activity to free the body and remove tensions in playing, and

5. A philosophy expressed in the text, *Nurtured by Love*.

The Suzuki approach is now applied to all string instruments, piano, and flute. For more information regarding the Suzuki method see the following:

SUZUKI, SHINICHI. *Nurtured By Love*. Exposition Press, Smithtown, N.Y., 1969.

KENDALL, JOHN. *The Suzuki Violin Method in American Music Education*. Suzuki Method International, revised ed., Princeton, N.J., 1985. (Originally published by Music Education National Conference, 1996.)

LANDERS, RAY. *The Talent Education School of Shinichi Suzuki.* Exposition Press, Smithtown, N.Y., 1984.

STARK, WILLIAM. *77 Variations on Suzuki Melodies—Technique Builders for Violin.* Summy-Birchard Music, Princeton, N.J., 1994.
The book is based on familiar Suzuki melodies and covers a variety of technical challenges involving double stop, vibrato, various bowing techniques, shifting, position studies, and harmonies. Included in the book is an extensive study guide that offers basic information and exercises to assist students in developing specific techniques.

SUZUKI, SHINICHI. *Man and Talent.* Shar Products Co., Ann Arbor, Michigan, 1990.

SUZUKI VIOLIN SCHOOL, 10 vols. Summy-Birchard Music, Princeton, N.J., 1995.

The Suzuki Association of the Americas, an organization that officially sponsors and approves many teacher training programs, may be contacted at 1900 Folsom, #101, Boulder, Colorado 80302.

THE ROLLAND APPROACH

Paul Rolland's approach was originally organized for the violin, but as concepts were developed, they were applied to other string instruments. The central premise of his approach was that movement training, designed to release the student from excessive tensions, could be presented from the incipient stages in an organized plan that would contribute to faster learning and better playing in all facets of instruction. His "action studies" culminated in a method book, *Prelude to String Playing,* published by Boosey & Hawkes and coauthored by Ed Krolick, a bassist, and Margaret Rowell, a cellist. A latter supplement to the *Prelude* is *Read and Play,* which is essentially a rote-to-note approach also published by Boosey & Hawkes.

With funding from the U.S. Office of Education, Rolland produced fourteen color films and, with Marla Mutschler, coauthored the book, *The Teaching of Action in String Playing.* In addition, the project also produced music, recordings, and photographs illustrating basic techniques that were introduced by Rolland through his research.[1]

Rolland believed that string teaching involved two important movements, the physiological and the physical. He defined physiological movement as the "functions of the body in play." Physical movements were concerned with "speed, weight of the moving arm and bow; starting, acceleration, deceleration, change of direction, [and] stopping of the movement."[2]

His visual materials and other texts may be obtained through the Illinois String Research Project, University of Illinois, Urbana, Illinois. ASTA has published *The Writings of Paul Rolland: An Annotated Bibliography,* by Mark Joseph Eisele.

KATÓ HAVAS

Although Kató Havas did not consider her approach to teaching the violin a "method," she did look upon it as a "system" utilized to organize the body's natural movement and balance for performing on the instrument. Her book does not contain music based on an organized structure of repertoire, but rather it offers detailed information on the application of how to apply her system to *all* students regardless of their performance level.

[1]Rolland String Research Associates, 404 East Oregon Street, Urbana, Illinois.
[2]Marianne Murray Perkins, *A Comparison of Violin-Playing Techniques: Kato Havas, Paul Rolland, and Shinichi Suzuki.* Reston: American String Teachers Association, 1995, p. 92.

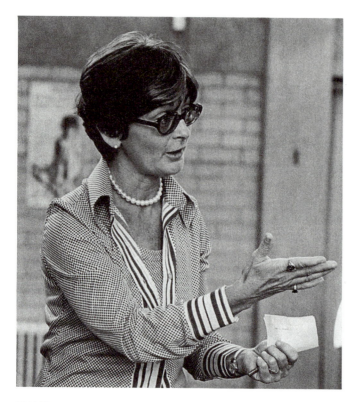

Kató Havas

In her early work, *A New Approach to Violin Playing*, Havas identifies five areas that are fundamental to her approach. They are: "(1) fundamental balances and movements, (2) the principle of 'inside-outside' playing, (3) the secret of the gypsy violinist, (4) the major causes of physical tension in playing, and (5) the major causes of mental tension in playing." Although Havas's work focuses on violin playing, she believes, along with her followers, that her principles and concepts of balance and mental application may be applied to all string instruments.

Publications by Kató Havas are:

A New Approach to Violin Playing. Bosworth and Company, London, England, 1961.

The Twelve Lesson Course, Bosworth and Company, London, England, 1964. (A series of exercises for developing technique.)

The Violin and I. Bosworth and Company, London, England, 1967. (An autobiography)

Stage Fright: Its Causes and Cures. Bosworth and Company, 1973. The book contains a thorough analysis of each of three factors affecting stage fright: physical, mental and social.

"The Release from Tension and Anxiety in String Playing," in *Tensions in the Performance of Music*, ed. Carola Grindea, 13–27. Kahn & Avrill, London, England, 1978.

In addition to these five basic books, Havas worked with Jerome Landsman to offer a sequential series of music for string classes:

HAVAS, KATÓ AND LANDSMAN, JEROME. *Freedom to Play: A String Class Teaching Method*. ABI/Alexander Broude, Inc., New York, 1981.

For an organized in-depth analysis of Kató Havas's system and her approach to violin teaching, an excellent resource is Dr. Marianne Perkins's *A Comparison of Violin Playing Techniques: Kató Havas, Paul Rolland and Shimichi Suzuki*, cited above. It may be obtained through The American String Teachers Association, 1806 Robert Fulton Drive, Suite 300, Reston, VA 22091. Her comparison of the violin techniques of these three seminal teachers is reproduced below.

Major Technical Features Compared

Techniques	Havas	Rolland	Suzuki
Foundation	Inter-related Balances	Balance & Movement	Listening & Imitation
Stance	Balance centered on "third leg"	Weight shifts between the two feet	Weight primarily over left foot
Violin Hold	"No violin" hold; scroll pointed just left of center of body	Balanced between six contact points; scroll pointed in direction of left foot	Supported by shoulder and chin; scroll pointed in direction of left foot
Violin Level	Slight downward slope	Eye level	Eye level
Bow Hold	"Flying bow" or "no bow" hold (Russian or Gypsy-style)	Traditional Franco-Belgian hold	Old German School hold (Joachim)
Right Thumb Position and Function	No set finger/thumb placement; thumb and horsehair link to transmit energy	Across from second finger; important for bow balance	Across from second finger; "Pan-da" Thumb Nail Action initiates tone and articulation
Right Arm Movements	Rhythmic divisions in the shoulder and elbow joints	Upper arm initiates bow strokes	Upper arm and elbow initiate bow strokes
Pronation & Supination	Some pronation and supination	Pronation and supination important	No pronation, no supination
Bowing Actions	Horizontal swinging movements	Rotary/cyclical	Convex arc patterns
Bilateral Movements	Yes	Yes	No
Bowing Path	A result of rhythmic arm movements	Varies according to music	Consistently on "Kreisler Highway"
Left Arm Movements	Left elbow swings away from violin	Left elbow swings under violin	Left elbow swings under violin
Left Finger Placement	Exclusive horizontal swinging actions	Vertical, horizontal (some), and across strings	Mainly vertical; limited horizontal
Vibrato	Non-traditional, "natural vibrato"	Traditional style	Traditional style; "two-toned" vibrato
Shifting	"Interval Swings"	Traditional ("Shuttles")	Traditional style
Tone Quality	"Unforced"; based on the "inner ear" and singing	"Full singing quality"	"Diamond Tone"; "Tone With Living Soul"
Miming Movements	Yes—fundamental	Some (bowing exercises)	Some (bowing exercises)
Singing/vocalizing pitches	Yes—essential	No	No

Reproduced, with permission, from *A Comparative Study of the Violin Playing Develped by Kato Havas, Paul Rolland, and Shinichi Suzuki*, by Marianne Murray Perkins, published by the American String Teachers Association.

THE BORNOFF APPROACH

George Bornoff developed a successful approach to teaching strings that focused on the left hand through the utilization of five finger patterns. When students became proficient in these five patterns, they were capable of performing music in any key at an early age or early stage of playing. Bornoff proposed that the entire finger-board be learned as early as possible, so that two fingered scales and other left-hand exercises were employed early in a student's instruction.

George Bornoff

At the same time, the student developed right-hand technique through a variety of studies that employed many fundamental bowing techniques almost from the beginning. These studies included up-bow and down-bow staccatos, spiccato, and détaché at varying bow speeds and utilizing the various segments of the bow. The function of these exercises was to build a tonal base that would result in a beautiful sound.

The initial books were all technical studies, but later songbooks were published to accompany the technical études. The songbooks utilized all finger patterns in a variety of keys. In addition, they used the bow techniques that students had acquired so that all their right- and left-hand technique might be used in a musical setting.

TRADITIONAL APPROACHES

Probably the most successful of all traditional books are the ones that were developed from string-class teaching by Sam Applebaum. The complete series of Applebaum books cover every aspect of string playing. They follow all of the established pedagogical procedures and contain popular folk songs as well as early, easy string pieces. The series is published by Belwin/Mills. In addition to his books and publications, which ranged from the very beginning stages of string playing to difficult, advanced studies, Applebaum developed a series of films designed to visualize ways of solving simple string problems. These films are also available from Belwin/Mills Publishing Corporation in Miami, Florida, in half-inch and one-inch video tapes.

Samuel Applebaum

Robert Klotman

Action with Strings by Robert Klotman, published by Southern Music Company, can best be described as an eclectic approach. It utilizes the finger patterns and bowing studies that one finds in the Bornoff books but is built around musical pieces that follow a sequence based on skill and technical development. The basic levels follow traditional patterns, and students acquire vocabulary and cognitive knowledge about music as they progress through the book.

CHAMBER MUSIC IN THE SCHOOLS

Every program, regardless of its grade level or the technical proficiency of its players, should offer opportunities for chamber music. Some of the benefits of playing one on a part are as follows:

1. It provides excellent opportunities for individualized instruction.
2. The listening skills of its participants are enhanced.
3. Exposure to one on a part helps players improve their melodic and rhythmic capabilities.
4. Players improve their intonation.
5. Through chamber music, students gain musical confidence and understanding.
6. All of these benefits contribute to the improvement of orchestral playing.

In addition, chamber ensembles offer the program considerable flexibility. Small groups may make appearances to enhance public relations where the larger group would be unable to appear. For further information regarding the use of and opportunity for chamber music, write to Chamber Music America, 545 Eighth Avenue, New York, New York 10018 (phone: [212] 244-2772).

STRINGS IN THE YEAR 2000

Music for orchestra represents a large part of the vast cultural heritage of the instrumental music of Western society. The genre includes works by the great European and American composers. All students should be exposed to this literature as well as jazz and non-Western musics. Young people interested in performing on string instruments should have the opportunity to pursue that interest and develop their talent.

Activities and Check List

1. What are some of the benefits of Strolling Strings?
2. Discuss the similarities and differences found in the techniques of teaching the violin as advocated by Havas, Rolland, and Suzuki.

PART III

Early Instruction

Holding the Instrument

Competency 4: Be able to specify and identify correct left-hand
position for holding your instrument.

Holding the Instrument

VIOLIN AND VIOLA

To acquire the proper playing position, the student should proceed
through the following steps.

1. With the strings of the instrument facing away from the body, place the
   left hand on the right bout of the violin and the right hand on the bout
   where the chin rest is located (see Fig. 3–1).

*Steps leading to proper left-
hand position on the upper
strings*

Figure 3–1

2. Swing the instrument into place on the left collar-bone with the button holding the tailpiece gut aimed at the "Adam's apple" (Fig. 3–2).

Figure 3–2

3. Turn the head to the left so that the jaw may drop comfortably into the chin rest. Get a sufficiently secure grip so that the left hand may be removed and the instrument still will be retained by the grip between the jaw and the collarbone (Fig. 3–3). To get the feel of this grip, it is sometimes advisable to substitute the fingers of the right hand for the jaw and press on the chin rest so that the student feels the support between the fingers and the collarbone.

Figure 3–3

4. Sight down the fingerboard and note that the scroll should be at the level of the tip of the nose. Whether sitting or standing, the student should be certain that his or her back is straight and his or her weight evenly distributed so that there is good balance at all times.

Left-hand position. During open-string rote exercises (see Fig. 3–3), it is advisable to keep the palm of the left hand on the right bout. However, once the fingers of the left hand are brought into use, the proper left-hand position should be established.

1. With the instrument held securely by the jaw and collarbone, move the entire hand back to the nut at the end of the fingerboard.
2. The neck of the instrument should be approximately at the first joint from the *tip* of the thumb. (This will vary according to the size of the thumb and fingers.) The base joint of the first finger should be level with the top of the fingerboard.
3. The thumb should be opposite the first finger or between the first and second fingers, as shown in Figure 3–4. (Some prefer it slightly behind or slightly in front. This will depend on the length of the fingers.) Of utmost importance is that the thumb and first finger form an open "C" so that the hand is free to move up and down the neck. The heel or palm should *not* touch the under part of the neck (see "Common Errors in Posture").

open "C"

Figure 3–4

4. The left elbow joint should be under the center of the violin. This will vary according to the string that is being played on and the length of the student's left arm. (It is desirable that the left elbow be pointed more to the right than to the left.)

It is not important whether the violinist or violist stand or sit when playing as long as he or she is standing or sitting properly. When playing in an ensemble, performers are usually seated. In private lessons or in a solo performance standing is preferable.

Standing position.   Most important is the position of the feet. They should be about 10 to 12 inches apart with the left foot slightly in front of the right, or the feet should be in line with each other. Basically, the body's weight should be balanced and equally distributed on both feet so that the performer can shift weight comfortably in either direction. Above all, students should avoid a rigid posture; they should be capable of moving in a flexible, flowing manner in whatever direction assists in proper bowing. (See Fig. 3–5.)

Figure 3–5

Sitting position.   When performing in a sitting position, the violinist or violist should sit on the edge of the chair with both feet on the floor. To avoid having the right knee interfere with the bow, he or she should move the right foot slightly back, raising the heel, thus lowering the right knee cap. Under no circumstances should performers be permitted to play with their

Figure 3–6

legs crossed. It interferes with proper bow movement and body balance. (See Fig. 3–6.)

VIOLONCELLO

To acquire the proper playing position for the cello, proceed in the following sequence:

1. Select a chair with a straight, level seat that will permit the performer to lean forward slightly. Avoid chairs that slope backward, for example, folding chairs.

2. Adjust the end pin so that when the instrument is placed between the knees, the upper rim of the cello at the neck block rests against the player's chest, just where the bones of the rib cage part (see Figs. 3–7 and 3–8). The corner of the lower bout is in contact with the left knee, while the right knee braces the instrument on the opposite bout as *it is tilted slightly to the right* (see Fig. 3–9). Both feet are generally flat on the floor; however, tall individuals with long legs may choose to bend the right leg behind them.

Steps leading to proper hold and balance on the lower strings

Figure 3–7

Figure 3–8

Figure 3–9

3. Check that the end pin rests on the floor in a line with the center of the body. The scroll should barely clear the student's left shoulder. It should not rest on his or her shoulder. A good reference point is that the bottom tuning peg is at about the left ear lobe when the head is held erect. (Be careful that the instrument is only an inch or two from the left side of the player's neck.)

Left-hand position.   The fingers of the left hand are virtually at right angles with the strings They should be arched with the thumb opposite the second finger. The thumb acts as a natural support for the arch of the hand, and its tip should be at about the middle of the neck of the cello. To find this position, use the following sequence:

1. Raise the left arm so that it is parallel to the floor with the palm facing down and the fingers and wrist relaxed.

2. Bend the elbow, bringing the ball of the thumb behind the neck of the instrument and the fingers over the string in an arched position. Roll the thumb slightly on its side, opposite the second finger to give support to the hand.

The cello left hand

3. Check the following:

    a. The elbow and wrist should be in a *straight* line with the fingers.
    b. The thumb should not grip the neck but should form an open "C" with the second finger (see Fig. 3–10).

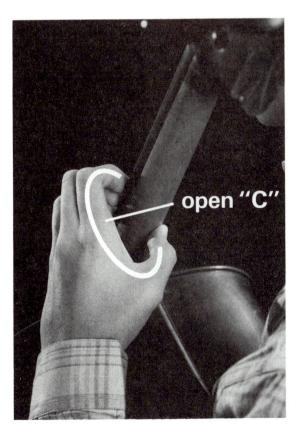

Figure 3–10

c. The fingers should be in an arched position just over the strings, ready to play each note.

d. Since the level of the strings over the fingerboard varies, the left elbow and forearm will change level as the hand moves from string to string (higher for the lower strings). In addition, as the hand moves to the lower strings, the thumb will also move slightly to the left of the neck of the instrument.

STRING BASS

The performer's body should be against the instrument in a manner that will permit the most durable position for bowing with the right hand, fingering the strings with the left hand. Neither hand should be favored when establishing position. It is of utmost importance that both hands be able to function appropriately without handicaps from inappropriate posture.*

To acquire the proper playing position, follow these steps (see Figs. 3–11, 3–12, and 3–13):

*The angle of the body in relation to the instrument will depend on whether the student is playing a French- or German-style bow.

Standing position for the string bass

Figure 3–11

Figure 3–12

Figure 3–13

1. Balance the body so that initially the weight is distributed on both feet. Hold the left side of the instrument with the left hand extended straight out in front, and center the instrument in front of the left foot.

2. Turn the bass a quarter turn to the right, and bring it toward the inside of the player's left thigh and knee. (The left foot may be placed on a rung of a chair or stool.) At the same time, turn the left foot at an oblique angle and bend the left knee toward the back of the instrument. The back edge of the right bout should rest against the performer's left groin.

3. Note that the bass is brought toward the player so that it leans against him. In this position it is balanced between the knee, the left thigh, and the abdomen, leaving the left hand completely free. The weigh should now be shifted to the right foot. (Many professionals use a stool when playing, as is shown in Figure 3–14. However, students *should learn to play standing.* Once the proper playing position is well established, they may use a stool in lengthy rehearsals; however, when doing so, they *must* employ the same principles learned when standing). Incidentally, the stool may be useful in teaching vibrato and shifting since it contributes to a more relaxed left hand.

Sitting position when playing the string bass

Figure 3–14

4. The nut at the end of the fingerboard should be approximately at the student's eye level, and the right arm should be able to reach comfortably the proper bowing position. (This will vary according to the student's height and arm length.)

5. Adjust the end pin on the bass so that it is at the appropriate height for the student. Another aid might be, when the left hand is in half position, it will be approximately opposite the performer's cheek. The right arm should be fully extended when drawing the bow across the strings. It should be straight but not rigid. (See Figs. 3–11 and 3–12.)

Left-hand position. The fingers of the left hand are virtually at right angles with the strings and are slightly arched over the strings in such a way that the fleshy pads of the fingers will fall in place on the strings. The inside corner of the thumb is placed against the neck of the bass opposite the second finger. The left elbow is *slightly* below the hand's level with the first finger acting as an extension of the forearm (see Fig. 3–15). The distance between the first and second fingers is the equivalent of one half step, while the space between the second and fourth fingers is an additional half step.

Figure 3–15

To acquire the proper posture, proceed as follows:

String bass—left hand

1. Raise the left arm so that it is parallel to the floor, with the palm of the hand down.
2. Bend the elbow and, without dropping the elbow, turn the hand and bring the ball of the thumb behind the neck of the instrument, with the tip of the thumb at about the middle of the neck of the bass and the fingers above the fingerboard.
3. Roll the thumb so that the ball rests slightly on its side, opposite the second finger.
4. Align the fourth finger so that it forms a straight line with the elbow. The first finger is pointed upward so that it appears to be aimed at the nose. The finger automatically moves down with the fourth finger.

Note that the thumb does not grip the neck but rests on it opposite the second finger, forming an open "C."

Since the level of the strings over the fingerboard varies, the left elbow and forearm will change levels as the hand moves from string to string. The thumb will also move slightly to the left of the neck of the instrument as the fingers move to the lower strings.

Activities for Violin/Viola/Violoncello/Double Bass

1. Observe yourself in a mirror and check to see if you are demonstrating the proper left-hand position on your instrument (violin, viola, cello, or double bass).

Self-Check List for Violin/Viola

	Yes	No
a. Is the *jaw* in the chin rest?	☐	☐
b. Are you able to drop your left hand and hold the instrument with the jaw and collarbone?	☐	☐
c. Is the instrument fairly parallel to the floor?	☐	☐
d. Is the left elbow joint under the instrument?	☐	☐
e. Are the left-hand fingers curved over the string so that the finger tips will be placed down on the string? (See Fig. 3–4.)	☐	☐
f. Is the thumb pointed toward the ceiling, opposite the first finger or between the first and second fingers? (See Fig. 3–4.)	☐	☐
g. Do the thumb and first finger form an open "C" so that the neck of the violin is *not* down in the web between the fingers? (See Fig. 3–4.)	☐	☐

Self-Check List for Violoncello

	Yes	No
a. Is the end pin at the proper height so that the neck block rests just where the bones of the rib cage part?	☐	☐
b. Is the end pin resting on the floor in a line with the center of the body?	☐	☐
c. The scroll is *not* resting on your shoulder.	☐	☐
d. When putting the left-hand fingers in playing position are they virtually at right angles with the strings?	☐	☐
e. Are the fingers arched, with the thumb opposite the second finger?	☐	☐
f. Are the elbow and wrist in a straight line with the fingers?	☐	☐
g. Does the thumb form an open "C" with the second finger?	☐	☐

Self-Check List for Double Bass

	Yes	No
a. Is the end pin at the proper height so that the nut at the end of the fingerboard is approximately at your eye level?	☐	☐
b. Are you able to balance the bass between your knee, thigh, and abdomen so that your left hand is sufficiently free to remove it from the neck? (Try it!)	☐	☐
c. When placing your fingers in playing position, are they at right angles with the strings?	☐	☐
d. Is the thumb opposite the second finger?	☐	☐
e. Is the fourth finger in a straight line with the elbow?	☐	☐
f. Is the first finger pointed upward?	☐	☐

2. Teach the left-hand position for your instrument to another student who does not play the one you are learning.

Holding the Bow

HOLDING THE VIOLIN BOW

Steps for learning the proper bow position for the violin and the viola are as follows:

1. Hold the bow on the screw with the left hand, with the bow hair toward the body (Fig. 3–16).
2. Place the inside tip of the right thumb on the stick against the corner of the frog.
3. Bend the thumb so that the upper part of it touches the hair. Whether or not it should touch will vary with teachers, but it is advisable to start with this concept to be sure that the *thumb is bent* (see "Common Errors in Posture").

Violin bow hand

4. Place the second finger opposite the thumb, with the stick crossing the crease in the first joint from the tip of the finger. Let the first finger fall on the stick across the middle joint.
5. Place the third finger comfortably alongside the second finger, with its tip pointing toward the pearl inset on the frog.
6. Then place the fourth finger in *an arched position* on top of the inner side of the stick. The fourth finger must be curved. In this position, the joints of the fingers are inclined toward the tip of the bow (Figs. 3–17 and 3–18). Be certain that all the fingers are curved and pulled "into the stick."

Figure 3–16

Figure 3–17

Figure 3–18

Figure 3–19

Figure 3–20

When placing the bow in playing position at the frog, the student should tilt the bow slightly with the hair toward the bridge at an angle. As the bow is drawn to the middle, the angle should be flattened so that from the middle to the point the full hair is used. As the point, or tip, of the bow is approached, the student should have the feeling that he is pushing the bow away from him. The process should be reversed when the bow is drawn from the tip to the frog. Note the angle of the left wrist in Figures 3–19, 3–20, and 3–21. Except on the cello (see discussion in the following section), the bow moves parallel to the bridge.

Figure 3–21

For "down-bow" on violins and violas, the left arm forms an imaginary triangle at the frog, a square at the middle of the bow, and then moves away from the body at the point. For the "up-bow," the arm merely traverses the return path, applying the same angles at the middle and frog.

HOLDING THE CELLO BOW

To acquire the correct bow position (Figs. 3–22 and 3–23):

1. With the left hand, hold the stick at the middle and parallel to the floor, with the hair facing the floor.
2. Bring the right arm up from the elbow so that the forearm is parallel to the floor, with the left hand hanging down and the fingers and wrist completely relaxed.
3. Place the right side of the thumb on the stick against the corner of the frog, and arch the thumb slightly. The middle, or second finger should be opposite the thumb, with the stick resting against the middle joint.
4. Curve the first finger slightly around the bow grip at the middle joint of the finger.
5. Then place the fourth finger approximately at the middle of the frog (where the pearl inset might be), with the first joint curved *over* the stick.
6. The third finger falls naturally in place beside the fourth finger.

Cello bow hand

All fingers on the bow are rounded and slightly separated. Avoid stiffness and tense, straight lines. The degree to which the fingers will fall in place or be rounded will be determined by the length of the fingers and the size of the hand.

Figure 3–22

Figure 3–23

The cello bow moves in an arc around the bridge as it moves from string to string (Figs. 3–24, 3–25, and 3–26).

Figure 3–24

Figure 3–25

Figure 3–26

HOLDING THE FRENCH BASS BOW

To acquire the correct bow position:

1. With the left hand hold the stick parallel to the floor, at the center with the hair facing the floor.

2. Slightly curve the right thumb and place the tip of the right side of it on the stick against the frog (see Fig. 3–27). It should be opposite the second finger, which is in contact with the bow at the second joint from the tip.

3. The first finger falls over the stick and curves slightly over the bow grip at the middle joint.

4. Drop the fourth finger over the frog at the first joint from the tip so that it hangs approximately at the pearl inset of the frog.

5. Allow the third finger to fall in place alongside the second finger (see Fig. 3–28).

String bass bow hand

Figure 3–27

Figure 3–28

The fingers are slightly spread and pulled into the stick. Raymond Benner of the Detroit Symphony suggests that one can accomplish a proper bow "hold" and "feel" if he imagines that the stick is like an archer's bow, with the stick being the bowstring. By holding the bow out with your left hand as if you were putting an arrow in it, and then pulling the stick with your right hand as if to shoot an arrow, you will obtain the proper position and the necessary curve in the right fingers for the "pull" utilized when playing.

HOLDING THE GERMAN BASS BOW

1. With the fingers of the right hand extended, place the screw section of the bow into the web between the thumb and the first finger.
2. Bend the thumb so that it lies on top of the stick and is turned slightly outward. Place the fourth finger underneath the frog, providing support for the frog, and allow the first and second fingers, slightly curved,

Figure 3–29

Figure 3–30

to rest against the side of the bow. The third finger rests in the curve of the frog (Figs. 3–29 and 3–30).

Activities and Check List for Violin/Viola

1. With the bow in playing position, turn your wrist over so that the bow hair is facing the ceiling and observe the following:

	Yes	No
a. Is the inside tip of the right thumb *on the stick against* the corner of the frog?	☐	☐
b. Is the thumb *bent*?	☐	☐
c. Is the thumb opposite the second finger?	☐	☐
d. Is the fourth finger (little finger) curved and on *top* of the stick?	☐	☐
e. Are the fingers inclined toward the tip of the bow?	☐	☐

Activities and Check List for Violoncello and French Bass Bow

1. With the bow in playing position, look in a mirror and observe the following:

	Yes	No
a. Is the thumb slightly curved and opposite the second finger?	☐	☐
b. Is the fourth finger *over* the frog so that the stick passes through the end joint of the little finger?	☐	☐
c. Are the fingers rounded?	☐	☐
d. When you turn the stick over so that the hair faces the ceiling, is the curved thumb against the corner of the frog?	☐	☐

Activities and Check List for German Bass Bow

1. With the bow in playing position, observe the following:

                                                                       Yes No

    a. Is the thumb bent slightly and on top of the stick and turned slightly outward?   ☐ ☐

    b. Is the fourth finger underneath the frog with the stick resting on the fleshy part of the little finger? (See Fig. 3–29.)   ☐ ☐

2. For all instruments, teach the bow-hand position for your instrument to another student who does not play your instrument.

Competency 4.2:   Be able to recognize visually common errors in posture.

Common Errors in Posture: Visual Clues

In teaching string instruments, it is essential to be able to observe errors by sight as well as sound. Careful observation may prevent poor playing habits and difficulties that might occur as the student progresses. The illustrations shown in Figures 3–31 through 47 are visual clues to improper body balance that causes tension, fatigue, and poor performance. Proper playing positions are shown on pages 49–65.

Visual aids in teaching

Improper angle of the bow.   Note that the bow is not parallel with the bridge (Fig. 3–31). This error is caused by a locked right elbow and wrist. Unless the elbow is opened up to move freely and the wrist moves down and out at the appropriate angle, the bow cannot move in a straight line.

Figure 3–31

Figure 3–32

Figure 3–33

Figure 3–34

In Figure 3–32 the left elbow is not under the violin and the instrument is much too low. The violin should be virtually parallel with the floor and the elbow sufficiently *under* the body of the instrument so that when playing on the G string of the violin or C string of the viola, the student may see the tip of the left elbow when glancing down the right side of the instrument.

Stiff fingers and thumb of right hand (Figs. 3–33 and 3–34). Notice how rigid and inflexible the fingers are. This locks the fingers and wrist and interferes with proper finger control. The student should work to *bend* the thumb and relax the fingers so that they are rounded and curve into the frog and stick.

Violin errors

Figure 3–35

Figure 3–36

Figure 3–37

Left-hand wrist "fold" (Figs. 3–35 and 3–36). This is a common error among beginners. It should be corrected by straightening the angle of the thumb so that it points up and by arching the fingers over the strings, keeping the wrist in a straight line with the arm and avoiding cramping and stiffness.

"Open palm" (Fig. 3–37). The wrist shown in the illustration is turned so that the fingers are not over the strings; this interferes with proper finger action.

VIOLA

All of the visual errors illustrated for the violin apply also to the viola. In addition, there are a few visual errors that can be observed when violinists change to the viola.

Viola error

In general, violists often hold their instruments slightly lower than violinists do in order to accommodate the larger, heavier instrument. Therefore, an adjustment must be made in the left wrist position. If the student holds the viola as in Figure 3–39, he or she should be instructed to make this adjustment, shown in Figure 3–38.

Although it is not always possible to see the adjustment in the right hand, there is a change, a shift in weight to accommodate the heavier strings of the viola. Some violins bend the first joint of the right thumb less than on the violin bow, in order to obtain a firmer grip.

Figure 3–38

Figure 3–39

VIOLONCELLO

The "violin bow grip" (Fig. 3–40).   This is a common error among students who have been taught by a violinist. The little finger should not be on top of the stick and the fingers should be nearly perpendicular to the bow.

Violoncello errors

The "violin left hand" (Fig. 3–41). Note the incorrect angle of the fingers of the left hand in relation to the strings and the neck. The thumb and the total hand position are affected by this error. The fingers should be perpendicular to the string rather than at the violin-playing angle.

Incorrect extension (Fig. 3–42). The abuse illustrated here is caused by improper understanding of the "backward extension." Although it is correct to make this extension with a backward movement, care must be taken to adjust the fingers and the hand by a compensating downward movement so that proper hand position is maintained.

Figure 3–40

Figure 3–41

Figure 3–42

Figure 3–43

Figure 3–44

STRING BASS

The "violin right hand" (Fig. 3–43). The little finger should *not* be on top of the stick, and the fingers should be completely realigned to be perpendicular to the frog. It is helpful for the teacher to suggest that the tip of the little finger be approximately where the pearl inset is on the frog.

Note also that the angle of the bow is incorrect. The bow should be somewhat parallel to the bridge.

The "violin left hand" (Fig. 3–44). Note the improper angle of the fingers of the left hand, and the total collapse of the joints of the fingers. Obviously incorrect as this seems, it is still a common error among students who are not taught by a well-trained bass player.

Improper height and angle of the instrument (Fig. 3–46). The bass is adjusted entirely too low, causing a poor left-hand position and improper spacing of the fingers. Figure 3–45 indicates improper angle of the bow.

When the angle of the instrument is incorrect, the student cannot cross strings properly, and his left arm moves awkwardly. Improper balance causes tension and fatigue and results in poor performance.

Often string-bass players are told to use their arms "like a pendulum," which creates the erroneous impression that the arm should be as rigid as the arm of a pendulum. The pendulum analogy causes the player to lock his elbow, and it should be avoided (see Fig. 3–47).

String bass errors

Figure 3–45

Figure 3–46

Figure 3–47

Activities and Check List

1. In a string class, check your stand partner or neighbor on each of the position items listed on pages 66–72.
2. Look in a mirror and check yourself on each of the items listed on pages 66–72.

Self-Check List

	Yes	No
a. When the bow is at the tip, is its angle correct?	☐	☐
b. Violins and violas, is the little finger of the right hand on top of the stick, with the thumb bent and opposite the second finger? Cellos and double basses (French bow), are your fingers perpendicular to the floor, and is the little finger over the frog at the first joint, with the thumb bent and opposite the second finger?	☐	☐
c. Violins and violas, check your left hand. Is it collapsed or in an open-palm position? If the answer is yes, then correct it.	☐	☐
d. Cellos and basses, is your left wrist in a straight line with your elbow?	☐	☐

Competency 5:   Be able to tune your instrument.

Tuning Procedures

TUNING THE VIOLIN, VIOLA, AND CELLO

One of the fears that people—children and adults alike—have concerning the study of a string instrument is the matter of tuning. It is important for the teacher to make a point of dispelling this fear at the very outset. For the youngster, especially, the teacher should tune the instrument (preferably in advance of the lesson, if practical) for the first several lessons or weeks. It should be remembered that the novice wants to play the instrument. He or she needs time to get the "feel" of the instrument and become "friends," so to speak, with the new music maker. After two or three weeks, the beginner should be ready to begin to explore, under the teacher's guidance, the process of tuning.

There are at least three approaches to tuning by the beginner that are in general use. Only one is recommended. It is important, however, to be aware of the other two approaches and understand why they are not acceptable.

Approaches to tuning

One procedure to avoid, if possible, is the direct string-piano method. In this method the student tunes each string to its equivalent on the piano; that is, the A string is tuned to the same A on the piano, the D to the piano D; the G to the piano G, and so forth. It is natural for the student to do at home what he has observed the teacher doing, and if one could be certain that the piano at home is in tune, this procedure would not be too objectionable. However, it is well known that the piano in the typical home is not usually kept in tune—at least not to the degree of accuracy necessary for tuning a string instrument. If the student tunes to a piano at home, he well very likely fail to get his instrument in tune. It is better that he use a good pitch pipe that possesses *the notes of all four strings.*

A second procedure, equally undesirable, is to tune the instrument to the note A on the piano, pitch pipe, or A bar, and then sing downward "sol–mi–do," or "5–4–3–2–1," or the first three notes of a song that begins with a descending major triad, and so arrive at the note D. Similarly, the student sings upward from the note A ("do–mi–sol," etc.) to find the note E. Experience has shown that relying on the voice in this way will seldom result in achieving a tuning in perfect fifths.

The procedure that is recommended is as follows:

1. Allow the student several lessons or weeks to become familiar with the instrument, with the way it sounds at close range, and, above all, with playing open-string double stops in exercises so that he or she learns the unique sound of a perfect fifth.

Desirable tuning procedures

2. At some point in the lesson, the teacher might sound the correct A on the piano, pitch pipe, or A bar, and while playing the instrument's A string, slowly turn the A tuning peg back and forth, thereby raising and lowering the pitch. The purpose of this procedure is to have the student listen and indicate when he or she thinks the two sounds produce a perfect unison. (To keep the true A sounding while the teacher does this, the student can stand at the piano and every few seconds press the A key.)

3. Once the correct A is established on the instrument, the teacher might play the open-string double-stop A–D, and by turning the D peg, slowly fluctuate the pitch. The student can then listen and indicate when the perfect fifth appears. This should be in the form of a game and can produce excitement and pleasure in a lesson.

4. When the student understands the principles involved and can identify the perfect fifth successfully, he or she is ready to experiment with these procedures alone, but still under the teacher's guidance. Much of the difficulty encountered in the early stages of learning to tune is the physical inability to maneuver the left hand while drawing the bow. Several kinds of nonslip pegs are now available, and they can be installed on any violin, viola, or cello. They immeasurably facilitate the task of tuning by holding their position wherever the student stops turning the peg (see Fig. 3–48). For some students it may be advisable in the earliest stages not to be encumbered with the complication of the bow. By holding the cello, violin, or viola between the knees and plucking the string, the student may simplify the process of pushing the peg into the peg box while adjusting the pitch, when regular pegs are used (Fig. 3–49). Bass students may also use pizzicato in the initial phases of tuning. On all string instruments it is better to loosen the string slightly and tune up to the pitch. *All steel strings must have tuners.* It is extremely difficult to tune steel strings accurately with pegs. Incidentally, tuning can and should be utilized as an ear-training exercise. The best procedure to tuning, then, is to focus on the interval of the perfect fifth for the violin, viola, and cello. String-bass students should learn to tune by

Figure 3–48

Figure 3–49

Tuning violin/viola strings

harmonics as early as possible (see page 76.) Good intonation is dependent on proper tuning. Learn to hear it! Learn to tune it! As a teacher, be patient but be definite in helping your students attain this accomplishment.

Self-Check List

    a. Match your open strings to your neighbor's.
    b. Violins and violas, recheck your open strings to see if you still hear perfect fifths with your left ear lifted away from the body of the instrument. Double basses and violoncellos, recheck for perfect intervals with the bow.

TUNING THE STRING BASS

Using harmonics to tune the string bass

The only acceptable way to tune the string bass is through the use of harmonics. There are several approaches to their use, but for accurate tuning, it is extremely difficult to rely on the open string. Once the student begins using the left hand there is no reason why he or she shouldn't experiment with finding the proper harmonics. Figure 3–50 shows the locations of harmonics on the strings.

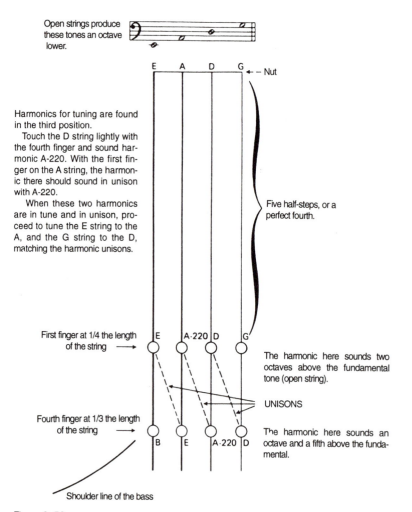

Figure 3–50

In tuning, the student should touch the D string lightly with the fourth finger at the note A (third position, or one-third the length of the string), where it will sound the harmonic A–220. The student should adjust this note to match the A given for tuning.

Once the D string is in tune, then, still in third position, the student should play the harmonic A on the A string with the first finger (one-fourth of the string length). Caution the student not to move the hand; he or she should stay in position and touch the string lightly to produce this harmonic. The A produced on the A string should then be adjusted to match the harmonic A on the D string.

When these notes are in perfect unison, have the student move the fourth finger to the A string and produce the harmonic E (third position—one-third the length of the string). By remaining in position and lightly touching the E string with the first finger, the student will produce the same harmonic E. The student should then adjust the note until the two sounds match.

To facilitate tuning the strings on a string bass, the strings are wound to a system of gears that make tuning much easier for this instrument (see Fig. 3–51).

The same procedure is used to tune the G string. Be certain, however, that the student adjusts the G string, not the D, since the D was the string originally tuned.

An appropriate guide to finding the fourth-finger harmonic is to be aware that it is located near the shoulder of the instrument (one-third the length of the string).

Figure 3–51

Ear Training

When tuning, students should sing the pitch for each string in order to hear the actual tone they are trying to attain. (After they have heard an A, having them sing a fifth above or below to develop an internal, aural sense of pitch will assist them in tuning.)

Silent Exercises to Reinforce Learning

Beginning students enjoy games.* The following may be useful to develop movement in the right arm and fingers. They may be used throughout the book.

Physical games to enhance learning

1. Exercise to develop freedom in the right arm:

   a. Ask the students to lift the bow and place it at the frog.
   b. Have them lift the bow and place it on the strings at the middle.
   c. Have them lift the bow and place it at the point.
   d. Once students have learned to distinguish frog, middle, and point, call out instructions of bow placement and begin mixing up the sequence (middle, point, frog, point, middle, etc.).
   e. In the beginning, work at a slow, careful pace. Then, since this is an exercise that may be used daily, gradually accelerate the speed of the commands until the students become proficient in the exercise.

2. Crawling exercises with the fingers of the right hand on the bow:

   a. Have the students hold the bow perpendicular to the floor, with the point aimed at the ceiling. Ask them to move their fingers from the frog to the point without moving the bow. When the students are fairly proficient in this exercise, continue as follows.
   b. Have the students invert the bow and aim the frog at the ceiling. Repeat the "crawling finger" exercise, this time moving the fingers from the point to the frog.
   c. Tell the students to hold the bow in the proper hand position (parallel to the floor), and without moving the stick, make their fingers crawl from the frog to the point.
   d. Have the students invert the stick, so that the point is in the right hand, and let the fingers crawl from the point to the frog.

3. The teeter-totter game:

   a. With the bow hand in position, give the command "teeter-totter." The students rotate their right wrist and turn the hand over so that the palm and hair face the ceiling. This gives the teacher and student the opportunity to examine the hand for proper playing position (see self-check list).
   b. Repeat the command "teeter-totter," and the students turn the hand back to playing position.

*Phyllis Young in her book, *Playing the String Game*, published by the University of Texas Press, describes games that are designed "To establish the concept of a beautiful tone. . . . To establish the habit of making tension-free motions. . . . To establish an attitude that is full of confidence and free of inhibitions. . . . To help the student learn how to study and to achieve a sense of accomplishment. . . . To help nurture a love for music and the instrument."

Activities and Check List

1. Play the teeter-totter game.* At the first command, with the palm facing the ceiling, check the following:

	Yes	No
a. Is the thumb against the corner of the frog and bent?	☐	☐
b. Are the thumb and second finger opposite each other?	☐	☐
c. Does the stick fall across the middle finger of the first joint?	☐	☐
d. Violins and violas, is the little finger *curved* on top of the stick?	☐	☐
Cellos and basses, is the little finger over the stick at the first joint and perpendicular to the floor?	☐	☐

2. "Teeter-totter" so that the bow is in playing position, with the palm facing the floor. Check the following:

	Yes	No
a. Violins and violas, are the fingers inclined toward the tip of the bow?	☐	☐
Cellos and basses, are the fingers perpendicular to the floor?	☐	☐
b. Violins and violas, are the fingers curved, with the little finger still on top of the stick?	☐	☐
Cellos and basses, are the fingers curved, with the little finger aimed or covering the mother-of-pearl insert in the frog?	☐	☐

*The game does *not* apply to the double-bass German-bow position.

Playing the Instrument on the Open Strings

> Competency 6: Be able to play with a variety of bowings on the open string.

For all string instruments, the open-string cycle offers an excellent format for bowing studies that are best taught by rote (see pp. 85 and 89). The cycle begins on the C string of the viola and the cello and progresses through a series of fifths (G, D, and A, played by all four instruments,) to the E string of the violin and bass. After repeating the upper string, it returns to the C. Once the cycle is established, the teacher may use any combination of notes or rhythmic patterns for rote instruction. (See the nine examples on page 90.) By varying the bow speeds and by using all sections of the bow in different combinations, the student builds up a tonal base and develops right-hand facility.

A student is primarily interested in producing sound, and sound production is one of the prime functions of the right arm. Early studies should be designed to develop coordination in the bowing arm.

Bow placement

The bow is drawn approximately midway between the bridge and fingerboard. The exact spot will vary according to where the best response or sound is found.

Introducing the Open Strings

The violin, viola, and cello are concert-pitch instruments that sound as they are written and are tuned in fifths. The string bass is also a concert-pitch instrument, but it is tuned in fourths and sounds an octave lower than written.

Violin.   The thickest string on the violin is the G string, and G is the lowest note of the instrument. The open strings progress upward in the following manner.

Viola.   The thickest string on the viola is the C string and the C is the lowest note of the instrument. The open strings progress upward in the following manner.

Violoncello. The thickest string on the violoncello is the C string, and C is the lowest note of the instrument. The open strings progress upward in the following manner.

String bass. The thickest string on the string bass is the E string, and this is usually the lowest *string* on the instrument, although special extensions make it possible for professionals to play lower notes. Beginning with the E, the open strings progress upward in the following manner.

Many different bowing studies, combined with the open-string cycle, should be employed (see pp. 86 and 90). The student should acquire a repertoire of bowings that can be utilized at various times to develop right-hand skills.

When the teacher introduces new material, the student should continue to use the pizzicato in banjo style or playing position, and then arco, although of course, this may not be appropriate for all exercises or bowings.

In addition, the student should experiment with finding the proper place between the bridge and the fingerboard for the most desirable tone. Although students are usually instructed to put the bow midway between the bridge and the fingerboard, the best point for beautiful tone will vary with different instruments. Determination of the best sounding point also changes with the speed and pressure of the bow and with changes in the string length.

Finding the tonal center

Competency 7:   Be able to play pizzicato.

Pizzicato

The Italian word *pizzicato* (abbreviated *pizz.*) indicates that the player is to pluck the string with the finger. This technique produces a unique sound effect; it also is useful in the early stages of learning to play a string instrument. By using pizzicato, the performer is relieved an any bowing problems while learning the notes of a piece. The following procedure is suggested.

Place the bow on the music stand. Now form the right hand as shown in Figure 4-1, with the thumb and first finger extended and the second, third, and fourth fingers curved into the palm of the hand.

Figure 4–1

Figure 4–2

Using Figure 4–2 as a model, place the fleshy part of the thumb against the fingerboard, with the first finger well extended over the strings, about two inches from the large end of the fingerboard on the violin and a proportional distance on the larger string instruments. At all times during early pizzicato playing, keep the thumb anchored against the fingerboard. This provides a base for accuracy in the selection of strings. To hold the string in plucking, use only the fleshy part near the end of the first finger. The pulling motion should be from the side, not downward. (Cellos see Figure 4–4, and bass players see Figures 4–5 and 4–6.)

If the entire piece (or exercise) is to be played pizzicato, the bow can remain on the music stand, thereby freeing the right hand completely. At other times, however, the bow must remain in the right hand. It can be held with the second, third, and fourth fingers, with the thumb and first finger extended. see Figures 4–3, 4–4, 4–5, and 4–6.

Pizzicato game
for individualizing instruction

The pizzicato technique is useful in many ways in class teaching. While working on a piece (or a special technical problem), the teacher might let each student take turns performing separately with the bow while the rest of the class plays pizzicato. This not only affords each student the challenge (and thrill) of appearing as soloist, but also gives the teacher an opportunity to study and evaluate the progress of each student. At the same time, all the other students are kept busy getting additional practice, which they welcome, since they know that it will soon be their turn to be soloist with the bow.

Figure 4–3

Figure 4–4

Figure 4–5

Figure 4–6

Another effective use of pizzicato is to give variety and length to a piece for recital or concert purposes. As soon as the class has learned three or four pieces, regardless of how short or elementary the pieces may seem, an appearance of some kind is desirable. This not only demonstrates to others (fellow classmates, parents, and teachers) the progress that is being made, but provides a tremendous incentive for individual practice. A simple piece of only 16 measures, for example, can easily be made into a full-length concert piece in the following manner: first time, tutti with bow (arco); second time, tutti-pizzicato; third time, solo or duet with pizzicato accompaniment; fourth time, tutti and bow. If the piece is in two parts, the possibilities for variety are even greater.

Activity and Check List

1. Practice going from arco to pizzicato and back to arco 10 times.

Self-Check List

	Yes	No
a. Is your thumb against the fingerboard when plucking?	☐	☐
b. Are you plucking with the fleshy part of the tip of the finger?	☐	☐

The Open-String Cycle

⊓ is the symbol for "down-bow." (*Pull* the bow from the frog to the tip.)
V is the symbol for "up-bow." (*Push* the bow from the tip to the frog.)

See page 81 for instructions on pizzicato. Pizzicato may be performed either banjo style or in playing position.

Bowing Studies for playing the open strings:

1. Use the middle of the bow.
2. Use the upper half of the bow.
3. Use the lower half of the bow.
4. Use all three sections of the bow, staccato.
5. Play the entire cycle "down-bow," returning to the frog after each note:

6. Play the entire cycle "up-bow," returning to the point after each note:

7. Play the cycle spiccato (bouncing bow — see page 186) with the lower half of the bow:

Activities and Check List

1. Name the open strings and put them in their proper place on a staff. (Check your text.)
2. Describe the following terms and symbols: ⊓, ∨, arco, staccato.

Swing Your Partner

Slovakian Folk Song

Gavotte Excerpt

F. S. Gossec

Bowing Studies on the Open-String Cycle

Bowing Studies:

a) legato
b) spiccato (see page 186)

A bouncing bow moves like a staccato except that it rebounds off the string instead of remaining on it. The bow arm should be relaxed as it moves in a rocking motion, with the bow striking at the bottom point of this movement.

W.B. pt. W.B. fr.   W.B. pt. W.B. fr.

Double Stops

Double stops are used to teach beginning students because they amplify the string tone. In addition, playing double stops helps to develop a desirable string tone, since it cannot be done without rubbing the bow against the strings. Beginners tend to allow the bow to slide, producing a glassy tone, but double-stop playing requires a good pull and push. Another advantage is that this kind of practice will eventually lead to smoother string crossings.

The Open-String Cycle for Double Stops

College Song

Folk Song

Finger Patterns One and Two

> Competency 8: Be able to play songs with a variety of bowings in the first finger pattern.

The finger-pattern approach enables students to begin playing in a variety of keys at the very beginning of their instruction. The fingers of the left hand are not locked in any one pattern and facility is developed through movement. Materials that utilize only one key or one finger pattern for extended periods of time create false concepts.

The First Finger Pattern

The major triad

Finger patterns are based on a five-note scale sequence on the open string. Thus, the first finger pattern is the tonic tetrachord of the major scale, beginning with the open string (*do, re, mi, fa, sol*). It consists of the normal progression of two whole steps, a half step, and a whole step. In addition to forming the first five notes of the major scale, this finger pattern seems to be the most comfortable, natural position for the fingers of the left hand.

On the violin or viola, the distance from one finger to the next represents either a whole step or a half step. For a half step, the adjacent fingers usually touch each other. For a whole step, the adjacent fingers are spread apart. Plucking and listening for the correct pitch will determine the exact distance between the fingers. With the instrument under the right arm (banjo style), place the fingers in half steps and whole steps on the string and determine the correct spacing while plucking with the thumb of the right hand.

The first finger pattern for the violin or viola is as follows (see Fig. 5–1).

Awareness of key is basic to music instruction, and instrumental training should develop the tonal sense. Students of string instruments should learn the vocabulary of music from the beginning so that it will be a part of their working knowledge and skills.

Figure 5–2

Figure 5–1

The second and third fingers, which constitute the half step (from *mi* to *fa*), practically touch each other. The degree of contact will vary according to the individual finger thickness and the string length.

On the cello, each finger represents a *half step.* To play a whole step at this stage, one must skip a finger. Thus, a whole step from the first finger would be the third finger. Since it is desirable to keep as many fingers as possible on the string, the intervening finger is also placed on the string.

The first finger pattern for the cello is as follows (see Fig. 5–2):

$$\overset{\wedge}{(0\text{–}1\text{–}3\ 4\text{–}0)}$$

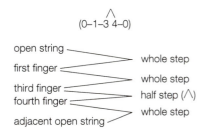

On the string bass, the span of all four fingers represents a whole step. The first finger pattern for string bass is as follows (see Fig. 5–3):

Figure 5–3

Activities and Check List

1. Place the fingers silently on the string in the first finger pattern. (Violins and violas, hold the instrument banjo style, watching where the fingers fall.)
2. Play the fingers pizzicato.
3. Violin and viola, do the above on all four strings. Violoncello and double bass, do the above only on the lower three strings.
4. Play the pattern arco.
5. Practive the first finger-patterns material on pages 96–98.

Self-Check List

		Yes	No
a.	Sing a major scale from the tonic to the dominant (do-sol) beginning with the open string. As you pluck each note when playing the first finger pattern, does each pitch match what you are singing?	☐	☐
b.	When step one is fairly accurate, play arco. Does each note match the notes you sang?	☐	☐
c.	Violins and violas, are your fingers perpendicular to the strings and slightly arched so that you are pressing down with the fleshy part of your finger tips?	☐	☐
	Violoncellos, are your fingers perpendicular to the strings and slightly arched so that you are pressing down with the fleshy part on the inside part, *not the tip,* of the finger?	☐	☐
	Double basses, are your fingers perpendicular to the strings with your first finger pointed at a 45-degree angle toward the ceiling and the little finger pointing slightly down toward the floor?	☐	☐

MUSIC EXERCISES AND PIECES IN THE FIRST FINGER PATTERN

1. Practice playing the above patterns pizzicato. Violin and viola players should practice them in banjo style as well as in playing position.

2. Experiment by placing the fingers in the first finger pattern on each of the other three strings of each instrument.

Do the entire exercise, including the bowing studies, on the G string. (String bass may do so with shifts or remain tacit.) W.B. is the abbreviation for whole bow.

*An extender indicates that the finger should be held down for the duration of the line.

Bowing Exercise on First Finger Pattern

Bowing Studies:

1. Spiccato at the frog

2. Staccato (upper half and lower half of the bow)

3.

4.
a) legato (middle of the bow)
b) spiccato at the frog

5.
a) legato (middle of the bow)
b) spiccato (middle of the bow)

6.
Return to frog on ⊓

7.
Return to point on V

8.

9.
fr. W.B. pt. W.B.   fr. W.B. pt. W.B.

10.

11.

Continue to employ these bowings whenever applicable, such as in new finger patterns and scales.

"ZIPPING"

As a student begins to use the fingers of the left hand, he or she tends to grip the neck of the instrument. To relieve this tension, several exercises should be employed regularly.

"Zipping," which is placing the second finger lightly on a string and just sliding it up and down the neck, producing a siren sound, is one device to prevent a tense grip. If a student is gripping the neck of the instrument, his thumb will *not* move freely. In violin and viola playing, zipping may also reveal how well the student is holding the instrument with the jaw. Unless the jaw is holding the instrument securely, the left hand is not free to move.

"TAPPING"

Another technique to improve hand position is to tap the strings silently with all four fingers of the left hand in various positions (first position, third position, etc.), or at various points on the different strings. This develops mobility in hand movement, which is so essential to proper string playing.*

These exercises should be done daily with other silent drills.

*See *Action Studies* by Paul Rolland, published by Boosey & Hawkes, 1978.

Chorale

Johann Sebastian Bach

It is of utmost importance that the proper portion of the bow be used for the maximum effect. The point or frog must be used as indicated in the music.

Hold Up Your Petticoats

Folk Tune

PART PLAYING IN THE FIRST
FINGER PATTERN

Ensemble playing is a highly effective means of developing independence in playing. Almost any combination of instruments may be used in a duet, trio, etc. The Humperdinck duet given here may be played by members of the same family (for example, as a violin duet), or it may be played by a combination of instruments, such as the basses on part I and the violas on part II. It is a good idea to experiment with every possible combination.

Excerpt from *Hansel and Gretel*

Engelbert Humperdinck

*U.H.—upper half of the bow; L.H.—lower half.

Competency 9:   Be able to play songs with a variety of bowings in the second finger pattern.

The Second Finger Pattern

The second finger pattern is based on the tonic tetrachord of the natural minor scale, beginning with the open string (*la, ti, do, re, mi*). It consists of the normal progression of a whole step, a half step, and two whole steps.

The second finger pattern for the viola and violin is as follows (see Fig. 5–4):

The minor triad

Figure 5–4

The second finger pattern for the cello is as follows (see Fig. 5–5).

Figure 5–5

Figure 5–6

The second finger pattern for the string bass is as follows (see Fig. 5–6):

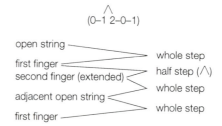

$$(0\text{–}\overset{\wedge}{1}\ 2\text{–}0\text{–}1)$$

open string ⟶ whole step
first finger ⟶ half step (∧)
second finger (extended) ⟶ whole step
adjacent open string ⟶ whole step
first finger ⟶

Activities for Check List

1. Place the fingers silently on the string in the second finger pattern. (Violins and violas, hold the instrument banjo style, watching where the fingers fall.)
2. Play the patterns pizzicato.
3. Violins and violas, do the above on all four strings. Cellos and double basses, do the above only on the three lower strings.
4. Play the pattern arco.
5. Practice the second finger pattern on page 108.

MUSIC EXERCISE AND PIECES FOR THE
FIRST AND SECOND FINGER PATTERNS

1. Practice playing the above patterns pizzicato. Violin and viola players should practice them in banjo style as well as in playing position.

2. Experiment by placing the fingers in the second finger pattern on each of the other three strings of each instrument.

Amaryllis

(First Finger Pattern)

Louis XIII (1601–1643)

*- means semi-staccato.

Self-Check List

		Yes	No
a.	Sing a natural minor scale from the tonic to the dominant (la-mi) beginning with the open string. As you pluck each note of the second finger pattern, does each pitch match what you are singing?	☐	☐
b.	When step one is fairly accurate, play arco. Does each pitch match the notes you sang?	☐	☐
c.	Violins and violas, are your left fingers curved so that you are playing on the fleshy part of your finger tips?	☐	☐
	Violoncellos, are your fingers perpendicular to the strings and slightly arched so that you are pressing down with the fleshy part on the *inside, not the tip,* of the finger?	☐	☐
	Double basses, are your fingers perpendicular to the strings with your first finger pointed at a 45-degree angle toward the ceiling and the little finger pointing slightly down toward the floor, in line with your elbow?	☐	☐

Slurs and Double Stops Using Patterns One and Two

Competency 10: Be able to play bowing with slurs.

Slurs

It is not uncommon to find that students may at first have a little difficulty in coordinating their hands and fingers when using slurs. To establish the concept of a slur (two or more notes on the same bow, i.e., the bow continuing in the same direction while changing notes), it may be best to begin by playing the open-string cycle with a short pause between each note. Once the idea is established, it is easier for students to combine the left and right hands in the use of slurs.

Two notes on a bow

Slurs (Open Strings)

Repeat on the G and A strings using the first and second finger patterns.
This exercise may be played as a round.

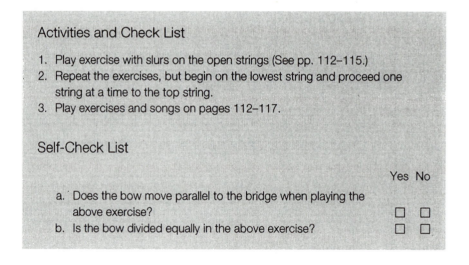

Activities and Check List

1. Play exercise with slurs on the open strings (See pp. 112–115.)
2. Repeat the exercises, but begin on the lowest string and proceed one
   string at a time to the top string.
3. Play exercises and songs on pages 112–117.

Self-Check List

	Yes	No
a. Does the bow move parallel to the bridge when playing the above exercise?	☐	☐
b. Is the bow divided equally in the above exercise?	☐	☐

Slurs (Three on a Bow)

Three notes on a bow

Slurs (Four on a Bow)

This composition utilizes combinations of the first and second finger patterns.

Bourrée

Johann Sebastian Bach

*Scales and arpeggios are the basis for most Western music. They serve as a medium by which most technique is developed, and they provide the best material for early ear training, particularly for establishing a sense of tonality. To make the study of scales more interesting, a variety of bowing and rhythmic studies should be utilized.

116

G-Major Scale. Two Octaves

Competency 11:   Be able to play double stops combining a finger
with an open string.

Crossing Strings and Double Stops

In the following exercise, the students begin to combine concepts. The first exercise involves "crossing strings," and it is of the utmost importance to keep the fingers down on the upper string through each crossing. This requirement is reinforced in the double-stop exercise, since the student cannot play a double stop correctly unless the fingers are kept down. In addition, the student becomes more acutely aware of intonation, since it is required to play a scale with a pedal point; the pedal tone must be kept constant, and each note of the scale must be tuned against it. When crossing strings, it is well to emphasize keeping the left fingers down as much as possible. This will not only facilitate a smoother crossing, but also will assist in developing better left-hand technique.

Because of the bowing angle of the violin and viola, which moves somewhat perpendicular to the ground, when going from a lower string to an upper string, begin with a down-bow. The cello and bass bows move parallel to the ground; therefore it is preferable, because of the arm and wrist movement, to begin with an up-bow when going from a *lower* string to an *upper* string. This applies mainly to a sequence of alternating notes, as in the next exercise. Do not forget, however, that we are applying this principle to *strings* and not to *pitches,* so that on the string bass the open G is higher than the open D and therefore begins with a down-bow.

Crossing Strings

Double Stops

Activities and Check List

1. Practice playing eighth notes in the middle of the bow, alternating open strings. (i.e., G-D-G-D, and so forth) Violins, violas, and basses begin with a ⊓ bow; cellos begin with a V bow.
2. Practice the above activity at the point and at the frog.
3. Play exercises on page 91.

Self-Check List

	Yes	No
a. As you play the above activities, does the bow remain parallel to the bridge?	☐	☐
b. Is the wrist on the right hand moving in a relaxed motion and not rigid or stiff?	☐	☐

Finger Patterns Three, Four, and Five

Competency 12: Be able to play songs with a variety of bowings in the third finger pattern.

The Third Finger Pattern

Introducing the extension in the cello

The third finger pattern is a scale pattern that begins on the third note of the major scale (*mi, fa, sol, la, ti*). Thus, the half step occurs between the open string and the first finger. Since this involves a finger extension for the cello, begin the scale pattern with the *upper note*, so that the player executes the extension of the first finger in a backward movement. (The octave is used to establish the correct pitch and to set the hand position as shown in Figure 7–1.)

Figure 7–1

This extension principle is essential to proper finger placement for the left hand on the cello. Too often heterogeneous string books introduce the first extension, the whole step between first and second fingers, by indicating that the second finger moves *down*. This is *incorrect*! In the beginning, the proper way to employ this whole step is a backward movement, or extension, of the first finger. In the process, the player drops the point of the elbow so that the hand is able to retain the same relative position and shape. The forward extension is another type of movement and is introduced later.

For the string bass (see Fig. 7–2), the entire hand moves one half step back, which lowers the pitch, and keeps the same finger relationship used in the first finger pattern, that is,

Half position for the string bass

0–0–4–1 0.

Figure 7–2

This, incidentally, is the half position for the string bass. (There is no "extended position" for the bass as there is for the cello. The normal hand position for the bass incorporates this extension.)

For the violin and viola (see Fig. 7–3), the interval spacing, beginning with the top note, is as follows:

$$4\text{–}3\text{–}2\text{–}\hat{1}\ 0.$$

Figure 7–3

For the cello (see Fig. 7–1), the fingers are spaced as follows:

$$0\text{–}4\text{–}2\text{–}\hat{1}\ 0.$$

Activities and Check List

1. Place the fingers silently on the string in the third finger pattern. (Violins and violas, hold the instrument banjo style, watching where the fingers fall.)
2. Play the patterns pizzicato.
3. Violins and violas, do the above on all four strings. Cellos and double basses, do the above only on the three lower strings.
4. Play the pattern arco.
5. Practice the third finger-pattern exercises and pieces on pages 125–128.

Self-Check List

	Yes	No
a. Sing a natural minor scale from the tonic to the dominant (la-mi) beginning on the open string. As you pluck each note of third finger pattern, does each pitch match what you are singing?	☐	☐
b. When step one is fairly accurate, play arco. Does each pitch match the notes you sang?	☐	☐

c. Violins and violas, are your left fingers curved so that you are playing on the fleshy part of your finger tips? ☐ ☐

Violoncellos, are your fingers perpendicular to the strings and slightly arched so that you are pressing down with the fleshy part on the inside, *not the tip* of the finger? ☐ ☐

Double basses, are your fingers perpendicular to the strings with the first finger pointed at a 45-degree angle toward the ceiling and the little finger pointing slightly down toward the floor, in line with your elbow? ☐ ☐

EXERCISES AND PIECES IN THE THIRD FINGER PATTERN

1. Practice playing the above patterns pizzicato. Violin and viola players should practice them in banjo style as well as in playing position.

2. Experiment by placing the fingers in the third finger pattern on each of the other three strings of each instrument.

125

Hatikvah

Israeli Song

Melody

Robert Klotman

F Major Scale

When playing chromatic passages, the violinist and violist will need to *slide* the finger indicated to the adjoining half step. Cellists and string bassists will use the appropriate half-step fingering. (It may involve moving the hand—shifting.) See page 123.

Chromatic Scales
(To be practiced separately in homogeneous groupings)

The Little Owl

Robert Schumann, Op. 79, No. 10

Competency 13:   Be able to play songs with a variety of bowings in
the fourth finger pattern (pp. 138–141).

The Fourth Finger Pattern

Violin/Viola

The fourth finger pattern is based on the tetrachord beginning on the seventh note of the major scale (*ti, do, re, me, fa*). It consists of a half step, two whole steps, and a half step.

On the violin and viola, to move from the third finger pattern to the fourth finger pattern, students need only lower the fourth finger a half step so that it touches the third finger. Thus, we have (see Fig. 7–4):

$$\overset{\wedge}{0}\ 1\text{--}2\text{--}\overset{\wedge}{3}\ 4.$$

Figure 7–4

Cello

For the cello, the fourth finger pattern involves a half step between the open string and the first finger, and it uses the same principle as established in the third finger pattern, that is, the fact that the extension is a backward movement. Note that there are octave jumps in the early stages of study in order to avoid use of the extended fourth finger, which later will be handled through shifts and advanced extension. See Figure 7–5.

String Bass

On the string bass, the same principle applies for the fourth finger pattern as for the third finger pattern (see Fig. 7–6):

$$(\overset{\wedge}{0}\ 1\text{--}4\text{--}\overset{\wedge}{0}\ 1).$$

Figure 7–5

Figure 7–6

EXERCISES AND PIECES IN THE FOURTH FINGER PATTERN

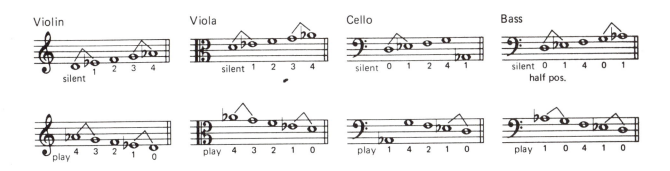

Practice playing the above patterns pizzicato (banjo style violin or viola) and arco.

Bowing Studies:

"Prayer from *Zampa*" (page 138) is arranged so that any of the string instruments, with the exception of the string bass, can perform it as a solo with a string-orchestra accompaniment. The accompaniment is supplied by independent parts, providing a full-ensemble effect. This kind of material is excellent for demonstrations at P.T.A. or administrator's meetings, for example.

Before playing this piece as written, practice playing it with a separate bow for each note.

Basses may play the Cello 1 line.

This material may be used for musical programs or for performances whenever the opportunity arises.

The C harmonic-minor arpeggio given here utilizes the fourth finger pattern. It is excellent preparation for the song, "Dark Eyes (page 140)."

C-Minor Arpeggios

Prayer from *Zampa*
(Solo for string ensemble)

Louis-Joseph-Ferdinand Hérold

Dark Eyes

Gypsy Melody

*Move the finger forward a half step.

140

*Move the finger forward a half step.

Activities and Check List

1. Place the fingers silently on the string in the fourth finger pattern. (Violins and violas, hold the instrument banjo style, watching where the fingers fall.)
2. Play the patterns pizzicato.
3. Violins and violas, do the above on all four strings. Cellos and double basses, do the above only on the three lower strings.
4. Play the pattern arco.
5. Practice the fourth-finger-pattern exercises and pieces on pages 136–141.

Self-Check List

		Yes	No
a.	Sing a natural minor scale from the seventh to the subdominant (ti-fa) beginning with the open string. As you pluck each note of the fourth finger pattern, does each pitch match what you are singing?	☐	☐
b.	When step one is fairly accurate, play arco. Does each pitch match the notes you sang?	☐	☐
c.	Violins and violas, are your left fingers curved so that you are playing on the fleshy part of your finger tips?	☐	☐
	Violoncellos, are your fingers perpendicular to the strings and slightly arched so that you are pressing down with the fleshy part on the *inside, not the tip* of the finger?	☐	☐
	Double basses, are your fingers perpendicular to the strings, with the first finger pointed at a 45-degree angle toward the ceiling and the little finger pointing slightly down toward the floor, in line with your elbow?	☐	☐

Competency 14:   Be able to play songs with a variety of bowings
in the fifth finger pattern.

The Fifth Finger Pattern

The fifth finger pattern is based on the tetrachord beginning on the fourth
note of the major scale (*fa, sol, la, ti, do*).

The intervals on the violin and viola are as follows (see Fig. 7–7).

*Second tetrachord in the
major scale: violin/viola*

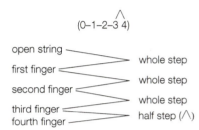

```
           ∧
(0–1–2–3 4)
```

open string	─
first finger	─	whole step
second finger	─	whole step
third finger	─	whole step
fourth finger	─	half step (∧)

Figure 7–7

Figure 7–8

The fifth finger pattern for the cello (see Fig. 7–8) is as follows:

Cello

```
           ∧
(0–1–2–4 0)
```

open string	─
first finger	─	whole step
second finger	─	whole step extension
fourth finger	─	whole step
adjacent open string	─	half step (∧)

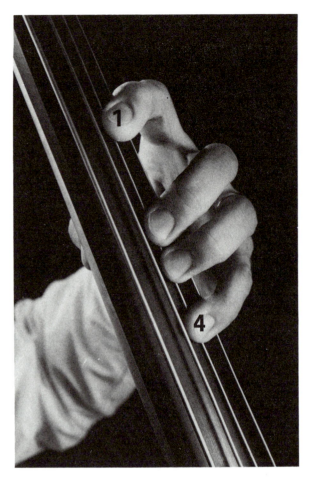

Figure 7–9   Figure 7–10

String Bass

In this pattern, the thumb of the left hand is in the same position in relation to the second finger as it was in the third finger pattern; that is, the first finger is extended backward.

The fifth finger pattern for the string bass (see Figs. 7–9 and 7–10) uses both the first position and the half position. Begin in the first position and move to the half position on the note that raises the open string. See the fingering given in the accompanying exercise on the A-major scale.

[0–1–4–1 (half pos.) 2].

Practice playing the above patterns pizzicato (banjo style) and arco.

EXERCISES AND PIECES IN THE FIFTH
FINGER PATTERN

Shenandoah

Activities and Check List

1. Place the fingers silently on the string in the fifth finger pattern. (Violins and violas, hold the instrument banjo style, watching where the fingers fall.)
2. Play the patterns pizzicato.
3. Violins and violas, do the above on all four strings. Cellos and double basses, do the above only on the lower three strings.
4. Play the pattern arco.
5. Practice the fifth finger-pattern exercises and pieces on pages 145–146.

Self-Check List

	Yes	No
a. Sing a major scale from the fourth degree to the tonic (fa-do), beginning on the open string. As you pluck each note of the fifth finger pattern, does each pitch match what you are singing?	☐	☐
b. When step one is fairly accurate, play arco. Does each pitch match the notes you sang?	☐	☐
c. Violins and violas, are your left fingers curved so that you are playing on the fleshy part of your finger tips?	☐	☐
Violoncellos, are your fingers perpendicular to the strings and slightly arched so that you are pressing down with the fleshy part on the *inside, not the tip* of the finger?	☐	☐
Double basses, are your fingers perpendicular to the strings with the first finger pointed at a 45-degree angle toward the ceiling and the little finger pointing slightly down toward the floor, in line with your elbow?	☐	☐

PART IV

Solos, Études, and Ensembles

Playing Solos, Ensembles, and Études in All Patterns

Competency 15: Be able to utilize all of the five finger patterns in a variety of pieces.

One of the best ways to promote a string program is to have beginners perform and demonstrate how quickly they can acquire enough skill to enjoy what they are doing. This helps to allay some of the concerns regarding the so-called extreme difficulties of learning to play string instruments. Performing solos is an excellent device for motivating students to practice. The Chorale from *Finlandia* on page 152 is arranged so that every member of the string class may be soloist with proper string accompaniment. This arrangement provides incentive, challenge, and pleasure for the soloist and for the entire class as well. The discipline involved in providing an accompaniment is helpful to students' musical development. It is important for them to learn to listen and to follow a solo line. *Finlandia* may also be played as an ensemble using various combinations of instruments.

Activities and Check List

1. Play pages 152–156. The first time through, have everyone play part I.
2. The second time through, divide the class or individuals into first and second parts.
3. The third time, switch parts.

Self-Check List

	Yes	No
a. If you are playing the first part, can you hear the second part in all the instruments?	☐	☐
b. If you are playing the second part, can you hear part I in instruments other than your own?	☐	☐
c. Are you observing the bowings as printed?	☐	☐

Chorale from *Finlandia*

Jean Sibelius

A-Minor Scale (Melodic)

Activities and Check List

1. The studies on page 158 explore further the bowing technique of spiccato. The spiccato is an off-the-string bowing motion that follows the same movement or direction as the detaché bowing (see p. 186). The arm is completely relaxed, however, so that the stick is free to bounce of its own accord. Once the "feel" of the stick's bounce is acquired, controlled bowings may be employed, following the scale pattern. In addition to those given here, students and teachers should create and practice bowing studies of their own, based on the scale.

2. The scale and bowing studies are to be used as preparation for "Farewell, Minka," a Russian folk song. The variations utilize different styles, such as legato, pizzicato, and hooked détaché, and the rhythms are designed to develop bow control and speed.

3. The theme-and-variation form is excellent for instructional purposes. It introduces variety into a repetitive idea. Students soon have the basic musical ideal fixed in their ears and minds. They can then concentrate on developing the skills required for each variation.

Self-Check List

	Yes	No
a. When playing the scale spicatto, is your arm sufficiently relaxed so that the bow practically bounces itself?	☐	☐
b. Are you practicing the scale with all of the bowing studies listed at the bottom of the scale exercise?	☐	☐
c. Make a cassette tape recording of your own performance of "Farewell, Minka." Does it sound enjoyable to you?	☐	☐

Farewell, Minka

Variations by Robert Klotman
Russian Folk Song

Trio from Symphony No. 39

Wolfgang Amadeus Mozart

German Dance

Joseph Haydn

Chorale

Robert Schumann

This is a review of combinations of the first, second, and third finger patterns. See directions on pages 92–94, 105–106 and 122–124.

Gavotte

Padre Giovanni Battista Martini

America the Beautiful
(Duet)

Samuel A. Ward

Theme from the "New World" Symphony

Antonin Dvořák

March from *Alceste*

Christoph Willibald Gluck

PART V

Intermediate Class Instruction

Some Simple Guidelines Determining Bowing

By now it should be evident that the string player's technique is in direct proportion to the development of his bow arm. All of the previous studies contain a variety of bowing exercises intended to free the right arm from rigidity and to develop correct phrasing and a good tone.

There are several schools of bowing, each taking an arbitrary position on its own advantages. Since the bow works either with or against gravity, and more strength is attainable close to the hand than at the point, we advocate the principle that more hair and greater pull can be applied as the bow moves from the frog to the tip. This idea comes from the Russian school, in which string players are taught to begin the down-bow using only part of the bow hair at the frog, with the stick turned so that the *hair is toward the bridge.* Then the bow is gradually turned so that the hair is flat against the string beyond the middle portion of the bow.

Basically, the turning or flattening is determined by the particular quality of sound desired, the distribution of the bow according to musical demands, and the stick balance. When selecting bowings for music, the player should be governed by technical and artistic demands as well as style, period, and taste. These criteria are important factors in the choice of bowing for a particular exercise or piece of music.

In performance a string player generally begins measures with a down-bow (⊓). Thus, if a composition or phrase begins with a single note on the last beat of a measure, the note is played with an up-bow (∨). A simple formula to follow is this: If there is an even number of notes before a barline, the player should begin with a down-bow; if there is an odd number, he should begin with an up-bow.

Accents are achieved best at the frog with a down-bow. Likewise, chords marked *forte* are more effective with a down-bow, but this, of course, will depend on the tempo and character of the music.

Since accents are played with a down-bow, unaccented notes are played with an up-bow, and consequently, afterbeats are frequently played with up-bows. The same basic principle of accented notes applies to syncopation. Since the accent falls off the beat, it should be played, if at all possible, with a down-bow:

Basic principles of bowing

On bowings that cross back and forth on the strings without slurs, the upper note should begin with a down-bow on the cello and bass but with an up-bow on the violin and viola. The reverse is true in those bowings that cross strings without slurs and that begin on a lower string; that is, the bottom note on the violin or viola begins with a down-bow, while on the cello and bass it is an up-bow.

When bowing is not specifically indicated, a combination of dotted eighth and sixteenth notes is generally played as a hooked bowing:

Incidentally, hooked bowings are used frequently to achieve many of the effects mentioned above; they permit the performer to arrive at the proper place on the stick so that he can anticipate and execute the next musical effect.

Competency 16:	Be able to describe and perform the following bowings: détaché, staccato, slurred staccato, martelé, spiccato, tremolo, hooked bowings, louré, sul ponticello, col legno, sul tasto, pizzicato.
Competency 16.1:	Détaché

Bowing Terms

DÉTACHÉ

Literally, the term merely means detached notes that are not slurred. In practice, it is the smooth change from one bow stroke to another. Often it is misrepresented as meaning strokes with a space between notes.

The détaché may be played at any part of the bow in a legato (smooth) manner. On the down-bow, the second, third, and fourth fingers pull the bow, while on the up-bow the first finger pushes the bow. To achieve smooth transfer in this finger action, the fingers of the right hand must be flexible and relaxed. An example of détaché bowing follows.

Activities

1. Practice each bowing on an open string as described in the paragraph that precedes it.
2. Practice the exercise.
3. Teach the bowing to another student.

Détaché

Wohlfahrt, Op. 45, No. 2

Self-Check List

	Yes	No
a. Do you feel the transfer of "push" and "pull" with the fingers, as described in the opening paragraph?	☐	☐
b. Is the dynamic level (forte) the same at the frog, middle, and point?	☐	☐

Competency 16.2:   Staccato

STACCATO

The staccato note is a detached, separated, or disconnected note played with the bow remaining on the string. There are many types of staccato; the style of music determines the type to be played.

A good rule for determining the duration of a staccato note is that it is one-half of its written value (written ♩ played ♪). A musical example follows.

Staccato

Rodolphe Kreutzer

Self-Check List

		Yes	No
a.	Do you hear the silence that occurs as you play each separate bow stroke?	☐	☐
b.	Is each eighth note of equal value in duration?	☐	☐

Competency 16.3:   **Slurred Staccato**

Slur (Staccato)

Self-Check List

	Yes	No
a. Do you have sufficient bow left to play to the last note of the slurred staccato?	☐	☐
b. Do you still feel the "bite and release" in the fingers of the right hand?	☐	☐

Competency 16.3.1:   Slur

SLUR

Slurred notes are those that continue in the same direction or follow in sequence without a bow change. The character of slurred notes may vary. It may be smooth, staccato, or even spiccato. See the following examples.

Slur (Smooth)

1. Staccato
(on the string)

2. Spiccato
(V V V off the string)

Competency 16.4:   Martelé

MARTELÉ

The martelé is a staccato stroke that is referred to as a hammered stroke. Each stroke must be prepared for by pressure before playing and must be followed by an immediate release of pressure. At the same time the bow is drawn quickly. The next stroke follows the same procedure—pressing, releasing, and at the same time moving the bow quickly. As in staccato, the bow remains in contact with the string at all times. Martelé, however, is more accented, and it is marked with a wedge (ı). The martelé is usually played with the upper third of the bow; the *grand martelé* is played with the whole bow. An example of the martelé stroke follows.

Martelé

Self-Check List

		Yes	No
a.	Does the bow remain at the upper third as you "hammer" each stroke?	☐	☐
b.	Is the bow moving fast enough so that you are using the *entire* bow when playing #2, whole bow and still maintaining the hammered effect?	☐	☐

Competency 16.5:   Spiccato

SPICCATO

The spiccato, a sharp staccato, is an off-the-string bow stroke. It is sometimes referred to as "bouncing bow." However, one must be careful not to assume that the bow is bounced like a ball. Actually, the spiccato bow moves in a horizontal direction like a détaché bow, except that there is a lift after each stroke, creating the bouncing effect. Occasionally, one uses a pure vertical motion for special effects.

There are two broad categories of spiccato notes, controlled and uncontrolled. On controlled strokes, the right arm is primarily responsible for the style. On uncontrolled strokes, such as *sautillé* or *ricochet*, the execution is a result of the natural tension and spring of the bow. The right arm is completely relaxed for all forms of spiccato bowings.

A beginning student should experiment to find which part of the bow is most resilient; this is the section that gives the stick its best springing effect. Examples of spiccato bowing follow.

Spiccato

Joseph Haydn

Competency 16.6:   Tremolo

TREMOLO

The term *tremolo* signifies the technique of moving the bow as rapidly as possible back and forth for the duration of the note value. It is best achieved at the point of the bow with a rather straight arm, but not rigid. To achieve the necessary speed of the stroke, primarily use the fingers and hand from the wrist. It may be played anywhere on the string—near the bridge, over the fingerboard, etc. Here is a musical example.

Tremolo

César Franck

Competency 16.7:   Hooked or linked bowings

HOOKED BOWING

The term *hooked bowing* is applied to the technique of tying or slurring notes to avoid awkward bowings or improper accents. An example follows.

Hooked Bowing

Hector Berlioz

Competency 16.8:   Louré

LOURÉ (portato)

The louré or portato style is a semistaccato type of bowing that is smoothly separated, or "pulsed." It is used to enunciate certain notes without pausing between them. To accomplish this type of bowing, a slight pressure is placed on the notes, as indicated in the musical example that follows.

Louré (Portato)

Antonin Dvořák

Self-Check List

	Yes	No
a. When making the separations in the above exercise, does it sound smooth and not staccato in character?	☐	☐

Competency 16.9:   Sul ponticello

SUL PONTICELLO

This type of bowing is done with the hair of the bow as close to the bridge as possible. To acquire the desired effect, it is helpful to tilt the bow hair slightly away from the bridge. See the musical example that follows.

Sul ponticello (German: *am Steg*)

Gustav Mahler

Self-Check List

	Yes	No
a. Is the hair of your bow against the bridge as tremolo?	☐	☐
b. Is it accomplishing the glassy effect you wish to hear?	☐	☐

Competency 16:10:   Col legno

COL LEGNO

Literally the term means "with the wood." In performing this type of bowing, the string is struck (or tapped) with the wood side of the bow. It is helpful to tilt the bow so that the hair is turned away from the bridge. Col-legno style is generally performed with the upper half of the stick. A musical example using this technique follows.

America the Beautiful

Samuel A. Ward

Self-Check List

	Yes	No
a. Practice moving the bow from arco to col legno silently. Can you do it comfortably?	☐	☐
b. Practice playing from arco to col legno on an open string. When you move to col legno is the bow hair turned away from the string?	☐	☐

Competency 16.11:   Sul tasto

SUL TASTO

This style gives a *sotto-voce* effect. It is performed with the bow placed over the fingerboard. The fingers of the right hand should be completely relaxed and hold the bow rather loosely. See the musical example that follows.

Sul tasto

Gustav Mahler

Self-Check List

		Yes	No
a.	When playing the above notes, is the bow over the fingerboard or on an open string?	☐	☐
b.	Do the fingers of the right hand feel relaxed?	☐	☐

Competency 16.12: Pizzicato

PIZZICATO

Pizzicato means literally "to pluck." It may be done with the right hand, or with the left hand if the right hand is occupied with bowing. Modern music may require "nail" pizzicato, where the string is plucked with a fingernail; "snap" pizzicato, which is achieved by plucking the string with such force that it snaps against the fingerboard; "thumb" pizzicato, which is accomplished by softly stroking the string with the fleshy part of the thumb; or the two-fingered pizzicato, used for rapid passages and also in order to avoid an arpeggio effect.

Pizzicato

Peter Ilyich Tchaikovsky

Self-Check List

		Yes	No
a.	Is your thumb against the fingerboard? (Although not essential, this is desirable for security.)	☐	☐
b.	Are you plucking over the fingerboard?	☐	☐

Competency 16.13:   Collé

COLLÉ

This stroke begins with the bow placed on the string similar to an up-bow spiccato. At the moment of contact, the string is pinched lightly but with a sharp attack. As soon as the note is sounded, the bow is immediately lifted off the string in preparation for the next stroke. An example follows.

Collé

Joseph Haydn

Self-Check List

	Yes	No
a. Are following the direction of the bowings indicated?	☐	☐
b. Are you observing the dynamics?	☐	☐
c. Listen to a recording of Haydn's "The Rider" quartet. Do you produce the same biting, crisp effect?	☐	☐

Competency 16.14:   Scordatura Tuning

SCORDATURA

A special scheme to tune the open strings in such a way that unusual effects, such as tone clusters, can be created by merely playing open strings. It literally means to retune the strings to pitches other than the established pitches and can be used in a variety of ways.

To Robert Klotman
O He Did Whistle and She Did Sing
(carol for children's voices in unison and two violins and cello, open strings)
by Richard Felciano

Player's Parts
(as they see them)

Activity and Check List

1. Create a composition for the class using scordatura tuning.

Self-Check List

	Yes	No
a. Did the composition have melodic, harmonic, and rhythmic interest?	☐	☐

Competency 17:   Be able to mark bowings in a string part.

Some Basic Bowing Guidelines

One must remember that none of these rules is binding. There are many exceptions that are dictated by musical concerns, and one can find instances where two outstanding string teachers will disagree over the same passage. These rules are merely set up to establish guidelines for the inexperienced string teacher.

1. Measures usually begin with a down-bow.
2. To comply with rule number 1, notes that begin before a bar line, if they consist of an odd number of separate bows, begin with an up-bow.

3. A dotted eighth note and sixteenth are usually linked. (See hooked bowing, p., 170.)
4. If there are a succession of uninterrupted sixteenth notes without slurs, then each group of four begins with a down-bow.

5. To achieve a crescendo, it is better to move from the point to the frog. (An excellent example of an exception to rule number 1, employing rule number 5, is Bach's "Air on the G String," which begins with crescendo on a sustained whole note. It is better to begin with an up-bow.)

6. Where long, sustained notes caused by ties, slurs, or tempo occur, it is better in orchestral playing to permit change of bow by different players at different times. On suggestion is: Do not change on a beat, and assign inside and outside players on each stand different designated times.
7. In syncopation, especially in accented or forte passages, the syncopated note is played with a down-bow.

8. When there is a tie or slur over a bar line, it is usually played with a down-bow.

Overture

Handel/Klotman

Moderato

Overture

Handel/Klotman

Developing Concepts to Accommodate Basic Orchestral Bowing Problems and Learning to Use Double Stops

Common Orchestral Bowing Problems

Problems in orchestral bowing may be divided into two main areas: (1) subdividing the bow length for proper phrasing, and (2) planning the bow stroke so that certain dynamics or a special bowing effect may be achieved. This does not mean to ignore such specific technical bowings as spiccato, staccato, and so forth; all of these skills require the development of certain techniques that are important in the second category mentioned above. If an orchestra director is prepared to handle both of the main problems, however, then all that remains is for the players to acquire the skills needed to execute the specific effect; this involves complications, such as bow speed, relationship of the bow to the bridge, and bow pressure.

Faults commonly found in the execution of bowing style are (1) too high a bounce or using too much bow for the various bouncing effects, (2) using too little bow for the martelé or the marcato styles, (3) general failure to relax the bow arm, and (4) playing entirely on the extreme edge of the bow hair.

In a performance, the main considerations for music interpretation are period, style, and musical effects. Both director and players need a knowledge of bowing techniques so that together they can produce a musical experience of value.

Double Stops

Double stops were introduced early in the study material as a technical device to accomplish the necessary "pull" and "push" for a full sound. In addition, double stops help develop correct ideas about the various right-arm levels and angles as one plays on different strings.

Frequently, when playing double stops, a poor tone is produced because the bow is not resting evenly on both strings. When this happens, the student is usually playing with more pressure on one string than on the other. (The double bass rarely uses double stops, but, even so, it is helpful for the bass player to practice these exercises, since they contribute to an understanding of correct bowing angles. See Figure 10–1.)

Building a tonal bass utilizing double-stops

199

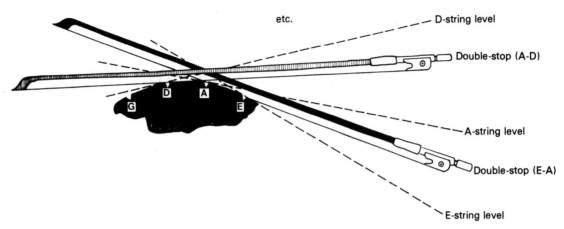

Figure 10–1

Learning to use double stops increases pitch perception. Intonation in orchestral playing is decidedly dependent on relative pitch, and double stops serve as a fine medium for ear training. However, in actual orchestral performance the particular string section is usually divided so that one group plays the top note, or group of notes, while the remaining instruments play the bottom note or notes (divisi).

The following musical diagram illustrates the use of double stops. (The violin strings are used to illustrate the principle. However, it applies to all string instruments.)

Competency 18:	Be able to play double stops using combinations of fingers.

Double Stops Using Combinations of Fingers

Activities and Check List

1. Practice the following exercise

Self-Check List

	Yes	No
a. When playing double stops, do you hear both notes in equal strength?	☐	☐

Double Stops

1. "Fingers on Top"
Note: The fingers are reversed for the string bass.

2. "Fingers on the Bottom"

3. Thirds and Sixths

201

Competency 18.1:   Be able to play double stops using additional combinations of fingers.

Occasionally it is necessary to play three- and four-note chords. These may be played in various ways, but generally as a two-note arpeggio, beginning with the bottom notes and followed by a double stop using the top two notes. As students progress, they will discover other ways of executing double stops; however, until they become proficient, they should follow the approach given below.

The following musical examples illustrate ways of playing of three- and four-note chords.

CHORDS ON THREE STRINGS

Three-note chords may be played in two ways:

1. As a broken arpeggio:

2. Martelé:

Press the bow firmly on the middle string at the frog and try to play simultaneously on all three strings.

Activities and Check List

1. Practice the following exercises.

Self-Check List

	Yes	No
a. When playing the chord, do you hear all of the notes in equal strength?	☐	☐

Competency 18.2:   Arpeggios

Arpeggios

The arpeggio is nothing more than a broken chord. The technique for arpeggios is similar to the one used with double stops, except that each note is played individually in the specified rhythm. (See the following musical examples.)

Arpeggios

CHORDS USING THREE AND FOUR STRINGS

Self-Check List

	Yes	No
a. When playing the chords, do you hear all of the notes in equal strength?	☐	☐
b. Are the intervals in tune or are you merely putting fingers down?	☐	☐

PART VI

Advanced Class Instruction

Explaining and Demonstrating Shifting into Five Positions

Competency 19:	Be able to perform exercises in the first five positions for each of the string instruments.

Position Études

The value of the material in this chapter will depend on the achievement level of the class. If the students are not sufficiently advanced for position studies, this chapter may be omitted or postponed for use at a later time.

As a violin or viola player progresses into the higher positions, he moves his left thumb and elbow under the neck of the instrument. The hand actually begins to follow the contour of the instrument when the performer goes beyond the fourth position.

The cello or bass player should keep the left elbow raised as he moves to positions above the fourth position.

As the distance between the bridge and the left hand is shortened, that is, in the higher positions, the bow must be drawn proportionately closer to the bridge on all string instruments.

Although this text presents the positions in numerical sequence in order to acquaint the college student with the fingerboard, in actual teaching it is better to use a classroom text that takes into consideration the problems inherent in each of the instruments. Some recommended texts are Applebaum's book for violin, Hans Sitt's or Sevcik's books for viola, Sebastian Lee's *Methods For Cello,* and Simandl's *New Method for the Double Bass* or *The Artist's Studio for Strings: Shifting Development Studies,* by Drew, Spinosa, and Rusch, published by Kjos Music Company.

Bornoff's *Finger Patterns in Position* is a book on all aspects of shifting for heterogeneous (all strings) classes. A violin student should begin position work in third or fifth position, using the body of the instrument as a guide to find the position. For the cello or bass, it is better to begin with the fourth position, where the same principle will apply.

The music on the following pages provides practice in various positions.

Competency 19.1:	Be able to perform exercises in the second position.

Position Études

1. Second Position

Repeat by rote on the D and G strings.

2. C-Major Scale in Triplets (Begin slowly with each ♪ = ♩)

*Positions are indicated by Roman numerals in these studies.

3. "Lovely Evening" (Second Position)
Play first in unison (as written), then as a round.

English Round

4. Third position

5. D-Major Scale in Triplets (Begin slowly with each ♪ = ♩)

6. "Lovely Evening" (Third Position)

Shifting

The chief function of shifting is to extend the range of the instrument. There are seven basic positions, plus variations added to accommodate modern fingerings; the string bass and cello also have intermediate (half) positions. For purposes of instruction, however, we will establish basic principles of shifting before exploring the fingerboard and its subdivisions.

Paul Rolland, a pioneer in analyzing movement in string playing, devised many exercises and organized these principles to promote freedom and mobility in shifting. Gerald Fischbach outlined them as follows in a series of articles for the *American String Teacher* (Summer/1980, Autumn/1980, Winter/1981), "Getting From There To Here with A Smile":

1. Shifting (and preshifting) activities should be introduced in the early lessons to encourage ease of movement and to avoid an artificial, learned fear of the upper region of the fingerboard.
2. Shifting activities should begin with large motions and refine to small.
3. At first, no specific pitch goals should be required. Progress gradually to specific points of departure and arrival.

To achieve a smooth shift, the left hand must be considered a unit that is free to move on the string. This freedom must be emphasized from the beginning of instruction.

One of the major obstacles to achieving a smooth shift is tenseness in the left thumb. To prevent this, it is helpful for the student to regard the thumb as an elevator that carries the hand when moving from a lower to a higher position. It moves at the same time with the hand and fingers.

Proper movement in shifting

The finger that is on the string when the student begins to shift remains on the string until the hand arrives in its new position. The finger that is to be used then falls into place, completing the shift. However, if the performer is moving to a new position, and the finger that is to be played is one lower than the finger initiating the shift, the finger that has a lower number falls into place while the shift is in progress.

All of the above motions must be practiced so that they can be accomplished with accuracy and in such a smooth manner that the various stages occur as though they were all part of one movement.

On backward shifts, the same rules of relaxation and freedom apply. However, it is the finger on the string that initiates the shift. Throughout, the basic relationship between the thumb and the fingers remains the same in the first four positions on the cello and bass, and the first three positions on the violin and viola. Beyond these positions, the thumb will pass gradually under the neck of the instrument as the hand moves to the higher positions.

A second function of shifting is for expressive playing. This involves the "portamento," which in effect is a slightly audible slide from one pitch to another. Since this can easily be overdone, it must be employed in a tasteful manner.

In the higher-numbered positions, the spacing between fingers is smaller.

In the third position on the violin and viola, it is advisable, for accuracy, to have the left wrist bend toward the body of the instrument so that the heel of the hand touches the body of the instrument.

The musical examples that follow are exercises for gaining proficiency in shifting.

Activities and Check List

1. Select a simple song from a songbook and perform it in a variety of positions, utilizing the concepts of shifting learned in this unit.

Competency 20:   Be able to explain and demonstrate principles of shifting.

EXERCISES FOR SHIFTING

1. Moving Between First and Third Positions (Same Finger)

Note 1: Each shift is preceded by an interval in the first position to establish the proper interval and pitch relationships.
Note 2: When making the shifts, glide on the finger that is down.

A considerable amount of the glissando sound that may be heard when the fingers are shifting can be eliminated by moving the bow slower and reducing the amount of bow pressure when changing position.

PURPOSE OF SHIFTING

1. Shifting extends the range of the instrument.
2. It facilitates technique by helping to avoid awkward string crossing.
3. It avoids awkward fingerings in passages.
4. It may be used for musical effects, such as retaining a desired tone color by staying on a single string in a musical phrase.
5. It may be used for an emotional effect, such as a glissando or portamento.

An excellent resource to supplement instruction in shifting is the "Guide and Videotape," *Joy of Shifting,* by Jessie Lucktenberg, assisted by Marvin Rabin, published by the University of Wisconsin-Madison Department of Continuing Education in the Arts, 610 Langdon Street, Madison, Wisconsin 53703.

Self-Check List

	Yes	No
a. Does the left hand move freely when shifting?	☐	☐
b. Are you able to move from one position to another comfortably?	☐	☐

2. Moving Between First and Third Positions (Different Fingers)
Note: (♪) indicates approximately the pitch where the shift ends.

a. Repeat in $\frac{2}{2}$ (¢) time.
b. Follow the same procedure on the A string.

3. Étude in the First Three Positions
   a. Slowly, with a separate bow for each note ($\flat$ = $\quarternote$)
   b. As written (𝐂)
   c. Gradually increase speed to ¢

Hans Sitt (Adapted)

216

4. Fourth Position

5. E Major Scale in Triplets

6. "Lovely Evening" (Fourth Position)

Competency 22: Be able to perform exercises in the fifth position.

7. Fifth Position

8. F-Major Scale in Triplets (Play slowly with each ♪ = ♩ at first)

Activities and Check List

1. Select a simple song from a songbook and perform it in a variety of positions, utilizing the concepts of shifting learned in this unit.

Self-Check List

	Yes	No
a. Does the left hand move freely when shifting?	☐	☐
b. Are you able to move from one position to another comfortably?	☐	☐

Teaching the Vibrato

> Competency 23:   Be able to explain and teach principles of vibrato on each of the instruments.

Another function of the left hand is to produce the vibrato. Many students are found to have a natural vibrato, and they should be encouraged to experiment with it. Some students, for a variety of reasons, however, find the vibrato difficult; placing undue pressure on them to vibrate too early in their development can be an inhibiting factor.

A smooth vibrato is continuous from tone to tone. Although a vibrato can vary in speed and intensity for musical effects, it must be even and consistent at all times, according to the type being utilized. Vibrato may be divided into three categories: (1) arm or forearm vibrato, (2) wrist vibrato, and (3) finger vibrato. The ideal vibrato utilizes elements of all three. It is important to avoid a tense, nervous vibrato that tends to stiffen the hand whenever it is used. Careful listening can best determine whether or not a student is producing a satisfactory vibrato.

Techniques for introducing the vibrato

Teaching the vibrato.   Many students acquire a vibrato by instinct. For those who need to be taught, there are many techniques that assist in the process.

For violin or viola, one technique is to rest the instrument against a wall (see Fig. 12–1), and, with the left hand braced in the third position, practice oscillating movements from the wrist using eighth notes, triplets, sixteenths, and thirty-second notes. Do this with each of the four fingers on various strings. When this exercise has been completed, move the hand to

Figure 12–1

the first position and practice the same rhythmic patterns, but adding the forearm to the movement. The combination of forearm and wrist produces the basic vibrato used by most performers.

The cello or bass player may practice the same *rhythmic* exercises for vibrato with a shaking back-and-forth movement. Because of the angle of the instrument, there is more of a shaking arm movement, with wrist and arm operating as a single unit, rather than the oscillating movement that is used on the violin and viola.

Under all circumstances the finger remains fixed; it should not slip or slide. However, this is not to say that rhythmic impulses do not project through the finger; it is in fact, this projection of rhythmic impulses that creates the vibrato effect. It is fundamental to understand that all vibrato begins where the fleshy part of the fingertip meets the string. The larger muscles of the wrist and arm then follow in motion.

When a student has difficulty acquiring the "feel" of a vibrato, it is helpful for the teacher to physically assist the hand with the rocking motion (see Fig. 12–2). Some violin and viola students are helped by going through the process with the instrument in an under-the-arm position and sliding the left hand back and forth as if they were polishing the string gradually reducing the area until the finger becomes fixed on a note. The function of this sliding motion, back and forth, is to create the sensation or feeling of the vibrato movement.

Assisting with the vibrato

Figure 12–2

Difficulties in producing a relaxed, even vibrato are usually caused by tension in the left hand that may result from the student either squeezing the thumb against the neck or gripping the instrument with the left hand rather than holding it with the jaw in the chin rest. To achieve a desirable vibrato, the left hand must be limp and the fingers flexible.

Figure 12–3

Cello and bass vibrato

The cello and bass vibrato is achieved by having the forearm and hand, from the elbow to the finger tip, roll back and forth in a wide arc. This rolling movement should be even and with as little effort as is possible (See Fig. 12–3.)

Musical exercises to provide practice in vibrato follow.

Activities and Check List

1. Practice the following vibrato etudes in the third position on all four strings, varying the rhythm as indicated below the exercise.
2. Practice the same exercise in the first position on all four strings varying the rhythm as indicated below the exercise.

VIBRATO STUDIES

Note 1: The ear discerns the highest pitch reached during the vibrato. To sound in tune, the vibrato must roll from the exact pitch to a pitch slightly below it and then back.

Pitch ∿∿∿∿∿∿∿∿∿

Note 2: Be certain that the thumb of the left hand is free of the neck of the instrument.

a. Do these exercises on all strings.

b. Do the same exercises in the first position.

c. Vary the rhythm:

Self-Check List

	Yes	No
a. With each different rhythmic pattern does the vibrato sound even?	☐	☐
b. Can you vary the speed from vibrato at different times and still hear it sounding even?	☐	☐

Teaching the Use of Harmonics

Competency 24:   Be able to play and explain natural harmonics.

In string playing, harmonics are divided into two categories, *natural* and *artificial,* and a single harmonic note may be produced in several ways in either of these categories. The effect of a particular harmonic note may be due to the use of a particular string, finger, or location on the string. Each method produces a different tone color; composers, writers, and conductors usually designate the method best suited to the effect they are trying to produce.

The tone produced when the bow is drawn across an open string is called the *fundamental.* The pitch of the fundamental is determined by the *nodes,* which are the stationary points at either end of the vibrating string; in the case of an open string, the nodes are the nut and the bridge. By touching an open string at the midpoint *lightly,* so that it is not pressed against the fingerboard, and drawing the bow across the string, a natural harmonic is obtained one octave above the fundamental.

The use of harmonics can help improve tone and intonation

Pressing a finger down *firmly* at the midpoint of the string introduces a new nodal point—the point of contact between the string and the fingerboard. Since the location of the nodes determines the fundamental, a new fundamental is produced. If one maintains this new nodal point with the first finger and touches the same string lightly at a different point with the third or fourth finger, the result, when the bow is drawn across the string, will be an artificial harmonic. Artificial harmonics may be produced by touching the string lightly at points one-third, one-quarter, or one-fifth of the way along the effective part of the string (i.e., the part bounded by the bridge and the nodal point maintained by the first finger).

When playing harmonics, it is a good idea to move the bow closer to the bridge than usual and apply the usual amount of pressure. There is a tendency on the part of inexperienced players to relax the pressure of the bow arm because they are touching lightly with the fingers of the left hand.

Harmonics may be introduced early in string instruction as a device to develop a good "pull" and correct use of the bow arm. Much will depend on the ability of the student and the teacher's background in proceeding at this level of instruction.

To indicate a natural harmonic, a composer writes the pitch at which the string is touched lightly and places a small circle above it; or else he indicates the place where the string is touched lightly by a diamond-shaped note. To indicate an artificial harmonic, a composer writes in the customary way the pitch at which the string is pressed firmly, and above it he writes a diamond-shaped note to indicate where the string is touched lightly.

The following musical examples illustrates the use of harmonics.

Natural Harmonics

Individual Sections

Note: On the cello and bass, for the natural harmonics in first position, one can produce different notes a third apart depending on whether one plays the note high or low.

Competency 24.1:   Be able to play and explain artificial harmonics.

Any note may be played as an artificial harmonic by placing one finger solidly on the black note that is notated and touching the same string lightly with another finger on the diamond-shaped note indicated.

Violin

Viola

Cello

Artificial harmonics are not practical for the string bass in the lower positions because of the string length.

Self-Check List

                                                                    Yes No

a. When playing the natural harmonics, do you maintain a full
    tone rather than a weak, squeaking sound?   ☐   ☐

Appendix

Special Projects and Assignments

1. There have been several successful approaches to class string instruction. Each one has its unique features and has been proved successful in a variety of situations. A competent string teacher should be well informed as to the various approaches and method books that are available, as well as their advantages and disadvantages. It would be a good idea, as a class assignment, to make comparative studies of some of the methods currently on the market. There are many more in addition to those listed below, but these are a few that have special impact on the philosophy of string teaching today.

ANDERSON, GERALD, and ROBERT S. FROST, *All for Strings*, Kjos.

APPELBAUM, SAMUEL, *String Builder*, Belwin-Mills.

BORNOFF, GEORGE, *Finger Patterns*, Thompson (Carl Fischer, selling agent).

DILLON, KJELLAND, and O'REILLY, *Strictly Strings*, Alfred Music.

ETTING, FOREST, R., *String Class Method*, Etling-Highland.

FARISH, MARGARET, and DON OWENS, *Shapes and Sounds*, Theodore Presser.

GREEN, ELIZABETH, *Teaching String Instruments in Classes*, ASTA.

HERFURTH, PAUL, *Tune a Day*, Boston Music.

ISAAC, MERLE, *String Method*, Cole.

KLOTMAN, ROBERT, *Action with Strings*, Southern.

MATESKY, RALPH, and ADELE WOMACK, *Learn to Play a String Instrument*, Alfred Music.

MÜLLER, J. FREDERICK and HAROLD RUSCH, *Müller-Rusch String Method*, Kjos.

ROLLAND, PAUL (revised by Sheila Johnson), *Young Strings in Action*, Boosey & Hawkes.

SUZUKI, SHINICHI (John Kendall-adaptation), *Listen and Play*, ZEN-ON, Summy-Birchard.

WIENIEWSKI, THOMAS and GEORGE HIGGINS, *Learning Unlimited String Program*, Hal Leonard.

2. Review periodicals

American Suzuki Journal, published by the Suzuki Association of the Americas, 1900 Folsom, #101, Boulder, Colorado 80302.

The American String Teacher, published by the American String Teachers Association, 400 South Lang Avenue, #1, Pittsburgh, Pennsylvania 15208.

The Instrumentalist, 200 Northfield Road, Northfield, Illinois 60093.

The Music Educators Journal, published by the Music Educators National Conference, 1201 Sixteenth Street, N.W., Washington, D.C. 20036.

Graded Materials List and Literature

The American String Teachers Association periodically publishes lists that are useful for the teacher. They appear in the *American String Teacher* or may be obtained from the office listed above or from 1806 Robert Fulton Drive, Suite 300, Reston, Virginia 22091-4348.

The Complete String Guide, ASTA, MENC, NSOA

MATESKY AND SMITH, eds.: *Orchestra and String Orchestra Literature,* ASTA

FARISH, ed.: *String Syllabus* (revised 1986), ASTA

The Music Educators National Conference has published a comprehensive listing of string orchestra materials, *The String Orchestra Super List,* edited by Frederick R. Mayer. This invaluable resource may be obtained for a nominal charge from MENC, 1806 Robert Fulton Drive, Reston, Virginia 22091-4348.

Suggested Materials for String Orchestra

A list of materials is obsolete the moment it is prepared. In addition, it is not feasible to select materials from a list or review without examining them. The following is a selective list to help teachers become acquainted with available sources. It is merely a guide to enable teachers to initiate programs.

KEY TO MUSICAL GRADE LEVELS

E = Easy:	For beginners in their first year and those beginning their second year. $(1-1\frac{1}{2})$
ME = Medium Easy:	Easy music for second- or early third-year students. Music may have sixteenth-note passages and accidentals, but is generally confined to the first position. $(2-2\frac{1}{2})$
M = Medium:	For intermediate students at the middle school or junior high school level. Music may contain early position work, spiccato and martelé bowings, and a variety of key and time signatures. $(3-3\frac{1}{2})$
MD = Medium Difficult:	For advanced junior high and high school students. It includes higher positions, many key changes, use of accidentals, and more varied bowings. $(4-4\frac{1}{2})$
D = Difficult:	Very advanced high school students and college students. Musical and technical demands are increased and a greater variety of bowing skills, as well as proficiency in fingerings and positions, are expected. $(5-6)$

Suggested Materials for String Orchestra

Composer-Arranger	Title	Publisher	Grade
Adler	Concertino for String Orchestra	G. Schirmer	ME
Adler	Four Early American Tunes	G. Schirmer	ME
Ahrendt	Pastoral	Ludwig	MD
Albert	Suite from "The Gift"	Shawnee	M
Alshin, arr.	A Little Klezmer Musick	Kendor	ME
Alshin, arr.	Nobody Knows the Trouble I've Seen	Kendor	ME
Anderson	Jazz Pizzicato	Belwin-Mills	M
Anderson	Plink, Plank, Plunk	Belwin-Mills	M
Applebaum, arr.	Music From Four Centuries for String Orchestra	Belwin-Mills	ME-M
Applebaum, arr.	Two Hungarian Folk Tunes	Belwin-Mills	ME
Avison-Isaac	Concerto in E Minor	Highland-Etling (Alfred)	ME
Bach-Dackow	Sinfonia in D Major	Ludwig	M
Bach-Isaac	Brandenburg Concerto No. 3	Alfred	M
Bach-Kjelland	Komm Süsser Tod	Highland-Etling (Alfred)	M
Bach-Leidig	Brandenburg Concerto No. 1	Alfred	ME
Bach-Levinson	Homage to Bach	Kjos	D
Bach-McLeod	Rondo	Kendor	ME
Bach-Ormandy	Three Choral Preludes	Boosey & Hawkes	D
Barber	Adagio for Strings	G. Schirmer	D
Bartok-Applebaum	Moods	Belwin-Mills	E
Bartok-Alshin	Six Bartok Miniatures	Belwin-Mills	ME
Bartok-Weiner	Ten Pieces from "For Children"	Boosey & Hawkes	M
Bartok-Wilner	Romanian Folk Dances	Boosey & Hawkes	MD
Beecher	Two Pieces for Young Strings	Shawnee Press	E
Beethoven-Isaac	Minuetto and Country Dance	Highland-Etling (Alfred)	M
Berger	Boulderollicks	Summy-Birchard	ME
Berger	short Overture for Strings	G. Schirmer	MD
Biber	Battalia	Kerby	M
Bizet-Isaac	Farandole from "L'Arlesienne Suite" No. 2	Highland-Etling (Alfred)	M
Bizet-Leidig	Carmen Suite	Highland-Etling (Alfred)	M
Bohm-Applebaum	Sarabande	Belwin-Mills	M
Bohm-Del Borgo	Perpetuum Mobile	Kendor	E
Brahms-Dackow	Serenade No. 1 in D Major	Ludwig	ME
Britten	Simple Symphony	Oxford Univ. Press	D
Bruch-Alshin	Scottish Fantasy	Kendor	M
Caponegro	Fiddling Around	Kendor	E
Cerulli	Four Dances for String Orchestra	Shawnee	ME
Chase	Simple Gifts	Hal Leonard	E
Chopin-Ettling	Two Preludes	Etling (Alfred)	ME
Corelli	Concerto Grosso, Op. 6, No. 3	Broude	M

Composer-Arranger	Title	Publisher	Grade
Dackow	Ukrainian Folk Songs	Ludwig	E
Dancla-Klotman	Herald Quartet	Belwin-Mills	ME
Dardess	Calliope (2. from "Concert in the Park")	Boosey & Hawkes	E
Dardess	Melody-Go-Round (3. from "Concert in the Park")	Boosey & Hawkes	ME
Debussy-Siennicki	The Girl With the Flaxen Hair	Highland-Etling (Alfred)	MD
Del Borgo	Dance Scenario	Kendor	ME
Del Borgo	Rustic Dance	Kendor	ME
Del Borgo	Two Welsh Airs	Highland-Etling (Alfred)	ME
Delius	Air and Dance	Boosey & Hawkes	M
Dello Joio	Air for Strings	Edward B. Marks Music	ME
Diemer	Pavane	Carl Fischer	ME
DiLasso-Klotman	Echo Fantasy	Fema (Wingert-Jones Music)	ME
Dvořák-Isaac	Three Slavonic Dances	Alfred	MD
Dyson	Knightsbridge March	Opus One	ME
Elledge	Copy-Cat Waltz	Kjos	E
Elledge	Phantom Dance	Kjos	E
Errante	American Folk Song Suite	Highland-Etling (Alfred)	MD
Errante	Ten Pieces for String Orchestra	Shawnee	ME
Fletcher	Folk Tune and Fiddle Dance	Boosey & Hawkes	M
Frackenpohl	Star Lake Suite	Boosey & Hawkes	M
Frost	Accents for String Orchestra	Kjos	ME
Frost	Backpackin' Strings	Kjos	ME
Frost	Fling for Strings	Shawnee	M
Frost	My Favorite Ice Cream is Chocolate	Kendor	ME
Frost	Pineapple Upside-Down Cake	Kjos	M
Frost	Rocky Mountain Switchback	Shawnee	MD
Frost	Tumbleweed	Southern	M
Gardner	Country Moods	G. Schirmer	ME
Gazda	Stringtown Stroll	Highland-Etling (Alfred)	ME
Gazda	Suite On Numbers	Kjos	E
Granger-Alshin	Shepherd's Hay (An English Morris Dance)	Alfred	MD
Grieg	Holberg Suite	Peters	MD
Halen	Stick Horse Parade	Shawnee	ME
Handel-Dackow	Allegro from Concerto Grosso, Op. 6, No. 2	Ludwig	M
Handel-Fisher	Entrance of the Queen of Sheba	Highland-Etling (Alfred)	ME
Handel-Frost	Fugue in F	Kjos	M
Handel-Siennicki	Little Fugue	Highland-Etling (Alfred)	ME
Haydn-Klotman	Midnight Minuet	Alfred	MD
Haydn-Klotman	Minuet and Trio from Quartet No. 20	Southern	MD
Hellem	Russian Peasant Dance	Kjos	M
Hindemith	Eight Pieces	Schott-American Music	D

Composer-Arranger	Title	Publisher	Grade
Hofeldt	*Kaleidoscope*	Opus One	ME
Holst	*Brooke Green Suite*	G. Schirmer	M
Holst	*St. Paul's Suite*	G. Schirmer	D
Horvit	*Invocation and Exultation*	Southern Music Co.	MD
Hovhaness	*Psalm and Fugue*	C. F. Peters	M
Humperdinck-Siennicki	*Hansel and Gretel*	Highland-Etling (Alfred)	M
Isaac	*Apollo Suite*	Highland-Etling (Alfred)	E
Isaac	*Early American Suite*	Highland-Etling (Alfred)	ME
Israel	*Dorian Variations*	Ludwig	M
Kabalevsky-Widoszynski	*The Clown*	Kendor	ME
Keuning	*Vistas De Mexico*	Southern	M
Kirk	*Hemis Dance*	Carl Fischer	MD
Kreichbaum	*Petite Tango*	Highland-Etling (Alfred)	E
Lassus-Klotman	*Echo Fantasy*	Fema (Wingert-Jones)	ME
Lichner-Applebaum	*Gypsy Dance*	Belwin-Mills	E
Lutoslawski	*Five Folk Melodies*	D.M.W.-Leonard	M
Marsh	*A Modal Festival*	Hal Leonard	M
McKay	*Port Royal, 1861*	Summy-Birchard (Warner)	ME
Mendelssohn-Alshin	*An Italian Elegy from Symphony No. 4 ("Italian")*	Alfred	MD
Mendelssohn-Frost	*Scherzo for String Orchestra*	Shawnee	M
Meyer	*The Bramble Hill Foxhunt*	Highland-Etling (Alfred)	M
Mosier	*Overture to the Wind*	Kjos	MD
Mouret-Leidig	*Rondeau from "Masterpiece Theatre"*	Highland-Etling (Alfred)	ME
Mozart	*Serenade, "A Little Night Music"*	Carl Fischer	MD
Mozart-Isaac	*Andante and Allegro*	Highland-Etling (Alfred)	ME
Mozart-Dackow	*Contredance En Rondeau*	Ludwig	ME
Nelhybel	*Danza*	Kerby	ME
Nelhybel	*Triptych for Strings*	Colin Music	ME
Nunez	*Apache*	Kjos	E
Nunez	*Déja Vu*	Shawnee	M
Nunez	*M to the Third Power*	Shawnee	M
Nunez	*String Swing*	Shawnee	ME
Pachelbel-Ades	*Canon for Strings*	Shawnee	M
Pachelbel-Caponegro	*Canon in D Theme*	Kendor	ME
Pancarowicz	*Paganini Variations*	MSB Publishing	MD
Peck	*Winter Music*	Belwin-Mills	ME
Purcell-Frost	*Two Seventeenth-Century Dances*	Kjos	ME
Purcell-Klotman	*Sonata in F*	Belwin-Mills	M
Purcell-Nelhybel	*Voluntary*	J. Christopher	M
Respighi-Alshin	*Antique Dances and Airs*	Kendor	M
Rimsky-Korsakov-Dackow	*Dance of the Tumblers*	Ludwig	E

Composer-Arranger	Title	Publisher	Grade
Satie-Klotman	Gymnopédies, Nos. 1–3	E. B. Marks (Leonard)	M
Scheidt-Klotman	Suite for Strings	Alfred	M
Schubert-Errante	Andantino and Allegretto	Ludwig	E
Shapiro	Folk Songs of Israel	Shawnee	ME
Shapiro	Matthew's March	Kjos	E
Shapiro	Minor Variations	Highland-Etling (Alfred)	E
Shapiro	Variations on a Ground	Kjos	ME
Sibelius	Andante Festivo	Southern	M
Siennicki	Cripple Creek	Highland-Etling (Alfred)	E
Siennicki	Country Dance	Kjos	E
Siennicki	First Suite	Highland-Etling (Alfred)	E
Smetana-Dackow	Country Wedding from the "Moldau"	Ludwig	ME
Smith-Isaac	Old English Dance	Alfred	M
Steg	Concertino Piccolo	Skidmore	M-D
Still	Danzas de Panama	Southern	D
Straub	Simple Square Dance	Boosey & Hawkes	E
Strauss-Isaac	Waltzes from "Der Rosenkavalier"	Boosey & Hawkes	MD
Tchaikowsky-Caponegro	Waltz from "The Sleeping Beauty"	Kendor	ME
Tchaikowsky-Dackow	Finale from Symphony No. 2	Ludwig	M
Tchaikowsky-Del Borgo	Serenade for Strings, 1st Movement	Kendor	M
Tchaikowsky-McLeod	Humoresque, Op. 10, No. 2	Kendor	ME
Telemann-Walter	Zwei Stücke	Shawnee Press	ME
Vaughan-Williams	Concerto Grosso	Oxford Univ. Press	E-MD
Von Weber-Dackow	Chorus of the Huntsman	Ludwig	ME
Wagner-Dackow	March of the Meistersingers	Ludwig	ME
Warlock	Capriol Suite	G. Schirmer	MD
Washburn	Serenade for Strings	Oxford Univ. Press	MD
Washburn	Suite for Strings	Oxford Univ. Press	M
Weinberger-Isaac	Polka from "Schwanda, the Bagpiper"	Alfred	M
Wiggens	Three Dances for Strings	Kjos	E
Withers	Fete Galante	Belwin-Mills	ME

Method Books

Author	Title	Publisher
Allen, Gillespie, & Hayes	Essential Elements for Strings ("Pop" acc. tape included)	Hal Leonard Corp.
Anderson, Frost	All for Strings	Neil A. Kjos Music Co.
Anderson, Frost	All for Strings, Theory Workbooks (1 and 2)	Neil A. Kjos Music Co.
Applebaum	Belwin String Builder	CPP-Belwin, Inc.
Bornoff	Finger Patterns	Foundation for the Adv. of Strings Educ.
Del Borgo	24 First-position Studies for Strings (Designed to assist in reading)	Band B Music Pub.

Author	Title	Publisher
Del Borgo	*12 Melodic Etudes for Application of the Developing Vibrato for Strings*	Band B Music Pub.
Dillon, Kjelland, and O'Reilley	*Strictly Strings*	Highland-Etling (Alfred)
Etling	*Etling String Class Method*	Highland-Etling (Alfred)
Green	*Teaching Stringed Instruments in Classes*	ASTA
Herfurth	*A Tune A Day*	Boston Music Co.
Johnson	*Young Strings in Action*	Boosey & Hawkes
Klotman	*Action With Strings*	Southern Music Co.
Matesky	*The Well-Tempered String Player*	Alfred Music Co.
Matesky, Womack	*Learn to Play a Stringed Instrument bks. 1,2, and 3*	Alfred Music Co.
Muller-Rusch	*Muller-Rusch String Method*	Neil A. Kjos Music Co.
Nelson	*Beginners Please*	Boosey & Hawkes
Nelson	*Spin-a-Tune*	Boosey & Hawkes
Rolland, Johnson, ed.	*Young Strings in Action, vols. 1, 2, and 3*	Boosey & Hawkes
Spinosa and Rusch	*Fine Tuning, 50 Intermediate String Ensembles for Developing Solid Intonation and Tone Production*	Neil A. Kjos Music Co.
Wisniewski and Higgins	*Learning Unlimited String Method*	Hal Leonard Corp.

String Orchestra Folios

Composer-Arranger	Title	Publisher	Grade
Applebaum	*Beautiful Music to Learn by Rote*	Belwin-Mills	E
Applebaum	*Chamber Music for String Orchestra*	Belwin-Mills	E-ME
Applebaum	*Concert Program for String Orchestra*	Belwin-Mills	ME
Applebaum-Paradise	*The Best of Haydn*	Belwin-Mills	MD
Applebaum-Paradise	*The Best of Mozart*	Belwin-Mills	MD
Cechvala	*Rosewood String Orchestra Folio*	Belwin-Mills	ME
Fletcher	*New Tunes for Strings, vols. 1 and 2*	Boosey & Hawkes	ME-M
Klotman-Burkhalter	*String Literature for Expanding Technique*	Fema (Wingert-Jones)	ME-M
Lieberman	*The Space-Age String Orchestra*	Alfred	E-M
Nelson	*Keytunes*	Boosey & Hawkes	M
Paradise, ed.	*The Best of Beethoven*	Belwin-Mills	M
Paradise, ed.	*The Best of Schubert*	Belwin-Mills	M
Paradise, ed.	*The Best of Vivaldi*	Belwin-Mills	M-MD
Siennicki	*Ensemble Time for Strings, bk. 1*	Highland-Etling (Alfred)	E
Vincent	*Baroque Album*	Highland-Etling (Alfred)	ME
Ward	*Concert Time*	Kendor	E
Zinn	*Henry Mancini for Strings*	Belwin-Mills	M-MD

Solo Music for the Violin

EASY

BIEHL-APPLEBAUM: *Hobgoblin Dance,* Belwin-Mills

BORNOFF: *Fun for Fiddle Fingers,* Thompson

CARSE: *The Violin Teacher,* Boston Music

FLETCHER: *Cornstalk Tunes,* Boston Music

FLETCHER: *Fiddle Dance,* Boosey & Hawkes

GARDNER: *Journey Through the Forest,* G. Schirmer

GIBB: *In Melody Land,* Broadcast Music

MELE: *First Adventures with the Violin,* Theodore Presser

O'REILLY, SALLY: *Fiddle Magic,* Kjos

SUZUKI, ed.: *Suzuki Violin School,* bks. 1 and 2, Birch Tree Group

TANSMAN: *Seven French Pieces,* Associated Music

WHISTLER: *First Etude Album,* Rubank

MEDIUM-EASY

BENJAMIN: *Tune and Variations for Little People,* G. Schirmer

BEYER-APPLEBAUM: *Dance of the Clowns,* Belwin-Mills

CAZDEN: *Four Favors, Op. 87,* Shawnee

KROLL: *Contra-Dance,* G. Schirmer

KROLL: *Donkey Doodle,* G. Schirmer

LICHNER-APPLEBAUM: *Gypsy Dance,* Belwin-Mills

MOFFAT: *Old Masters for Young Players,* Associated Music

MOSKOWSKI-APPLEBAUM: *Spanish Dance,* Belwin-Mills

MOZART-APPLEBAUM: *A Viennese Sonatina,* Belwin-Mills

O'REILLY, SALLY: *Fiddle Rhythms,* Kjos

PERLMAN: *Indian Concertino,* Carl Fisher

REIDING: *Concertino, Op. 36, D Major,* Belwin-Mills

MEDIUM

BAKALEINKOFF: *Gavotte,* Belwin-Mills

BARTÓK: *Hungarian Folk Songs,* from "For Children," EMB

BEETHOVEN: *Country Dances,* Oxford University Press

DYER: *In the Row,* Belwin-Mills

DYER: *Tempo Di Gavotta,* Belwin-Mills

GREEN: *Playful Rondo,* Willis Music

HANDEL: *Bourrée and Hornpipe,* Schott & Co.

HEIDEN: *Sonatina,* AMP

HUBER-KLOTMAN: *Concertino No. 4,* Carl Fischer

KUCHLER: *Concertino, Op. 11,* Century Music

LICHNER-APPLEBAUM: *Gypsy Dance,* Belwin-Mills

MENDELSSOHN, L.-KLOTMAN: *Student Concerto,* Carl Fischer (with orchestra accompaniment)

ORTIZ: *Dulce Memoire,* Music Corporation of America

PROKOFIEFF-FROST: *Lieutenant Kije's Wedding,* Edition Musicus

RAVEL-MAGANINI: *Pavane,* Edition Musicus

ROLLAND-FLETCHER: *First Perpetual Motion,* Belwin-Mills

SCHUBERT-APPLEBAUM: *Marche Militaire,* Belwin-Mills

SEITZ-KLOTMAN: *Concerto No. 4,* Belwin-Mills

THIRD POSITION

BOHN: *Sarabande in G Minor,* Carl Fischer

FLETCHER: *New Tunes for Strings,* vol. 2, Boosey & Hawkes

HANDEL: *Gavotte,* Elkan Music

HUBER: *Concerto No. 2,* Carl Fischer

PROKOFIEFF-LIPEMANN: *Three Pieces from "Music for Children,"* G. Schirmer

RIEDING: *Concertino 1, Op. 21,* Belwin-Mills

SCHUBERT: *Three Sonatines,* Associated Music

SEITZ: *Concerto No. 2,* Carl Fischer

SETIZ-KLOTMAN: *Student Concerto,* First Movement from No. 5 in D Major (available with orchestra accompaniment), Belwin-Mills

TEN HAVE: *Allegro Brillante,* G. Schirmer

ADDITIONAL REPERTOIRE FOR BUILDING MUSICIANSHIP

ACCOLAY: *Concerto in A Minor,* Southern Music (with orchestra accompaniment); Carl Fischer

APPLEBAUM: *20 Progressive Solos for String Instruments,* Belwin-Mills

CORELLI: *Sonatas,* Associated Music

DANCLA: *Six Airs Variés,* bk. 1, G. Schirmer

FRANCOEUR-KREISLER: *Siciliano et Rigaudon,* Charles Foley

GRANADO-KREISLER: *Spanish Dance,* Charles Foley

KRIESLER: *Liebeslied,* Charles Foley

KUCHLER: *Concerto in C Major, Op. 15,* Belwin-Mills

MACDOWELL-HARTMANN: *To a Wild Rose,* Schmidt (Summy-Birchard)

MURRAY AND TATE: *More Tunes for My Violin,* Boosey & Hawkes

PRACHT: *Twelve Easy Pieces,* Boston Music

SUZUKI: *Suzuki Violin School,* vols. 1–5, Summy-Birchard

VIVALDI: *Concerto in A Minor,* Associated Music

FIDDLING

Composer-Arranger	Title	Publisher	Grade
——	*Cajun Dance Hall-Special Fiddle Edition*	Mel Bay Pub.	ME to M
Chase	*Ragtime Fiddle*	Hal Leonard Corp.	M
Duncan	*Blue Fiddling Classics*	Mel Bay Pub.	M

Composer-Arranger	Title	Publisher	Grade
Duncan	*You Can Teach Yourself Fiddling*	Mel Bay Pub.	ME-M
Fiel	*The Essential Texas Fiddle:*	Mel Bay Pub. & Texas	
Greenblatt	*The Singing Fiddler's Tune Book*	Mel Bay Pub.	ME
Nunez	*Bluegrass Country*	Shawnee Press, Inc.	M
——	*Improvisation, Harmony, and Style*	Tech. Univ. Press	M
O'Reilly, S.	*Fiddle Magic—180 Technical Exercises for the Violin*	Kjos Music Co.	ME
Orme	*The Fiddlin' Workshop*	Mel Bay Pub.	ME
Phillips	*Mel Bay's Complete Country Fiddles*	Mel Bay Pub.	M to MD

JAZZ AND OTHER MUSIC

Composer-Arranger	Title	Publisher	Grade
Asch and Reiner	*Anthology of Jazz Violin Styles*	Mel Bay Pub., Inc.	MD
Abell	*Jazz Violin Studies*	Mel Bay Pub., Inc.	M
Bach-Kjelland	*Fugue in A Minor (Swingle Singers Style)*	Highland-Etling (Alfred)	M
Baker	*An Organized Approach to Jazz Improvisation for the Cello*	Jamey Abersold Jazz, Inc.	M
Baker	*An Organized Approach to Jazz Improvisation for the Violin*	Jamey Abersold Jazz, Inc.	M
Baker	*Jazz Suite for Violin and Piano*	MMB Music, Inc.	D
Biletzky	*Nocturne ("Slow Rock"-String Orchestra & Drum Set)*	Highland-Etling (Alfred)	E
Chase	*Bluegrass Bingo (String Orchestra)*	Hal Leonard Corp.	E
Chase	*Blue Ridge Boogie (String Orchestra)*	Hal Leonard Corp.	E
Cuellar	*15 Popular String Solos (For Violin, Viola, Cello, and String Bass, with accompaniment cassette for all 4)*	CPP-Belwin, Inc.	ME
Guest	*Gospel Violin*	Mel Bay Pub.	ME
Halen	*Fiddle Rags for String Orchestra*	Shawnee Press, Inc.	MD
Isaac	*Lazy Blues Suite (String Orchestra)*	Wynn	M
Isaac, arr.	*When the Saints Go Marching In*	Highland-Etling (Alfred)	M
Joplin-Buchtel	*The Entertainer (String Orchestra)*	Kjos	M
Joplin-Higgens	*Ragtime Dance (String Orchestra)*	Belwin-Mills	M
Meyer	*Moonlight Tango (String Orchestra)*	Highland-Etling (Alfred)	ME
Snell-Keith, arr.	*Favorite Latin Standards for Violin Solos, Duets, and Trios*	CPP-Belwin, Inc.	ME-M
Tiffault	*Hoedown Blues: (Country and Blues-String Orchestra)*	Highland-Etling (Alfred)	M
Tiffault	*Jazz Suite No. 2 (String Orchestra & Rhythm)*	Alfred	ME
Villoldo and Rodriguez-Isaac	*Two South American Tangos (String Orchestra)*	Alfred	M

Solo Music for the Viola

There are literally hundreds of excellent solos of all grades of difficulty. Except for those of artist grade, sonatas and concerti of intermediate grade for students are not so plentiful and are largely transcriptions. Nearly all the violin études are transcribed for viola. Many viola parts adapted to string-class methods may be used for individual teaching. The following lists are arranged in order of difficulty.

Solos with Piano Accompaniment

FIRST POSITION

ALETTER: *Melodie*, Carl Fischer

BACH-JOHNSTON: *Three Pieces*, Belwin-Mills

BAY, ed.: *Fun with the Viola*, Mel Bay

BERIOT-APPLEBAUM: *Serenade*, Belwin-Mills

COLLEDGE, K. & H.: *Stepping Stones*, Boosey & Hawkes

DUNHILL: *The Willow Brook*, Belwin-Mills

DYER: *Old Redcoat*, Belwin-Mills

DYER: *On the Serpentine*, Belwin-Mills

GOSSEC: *Gavotte*, Carl Fischer

HARRISON: *Amazing Solos for Viola and Keyboard*, Boosey & Hawkes

HAUSER: *Berceuse*, Carl Fischer

MÜLLER: *Andante Contabile*, Kjos

NELSON: *Piece by Piece*, Boosey & Hawkes

NELSON: *Right from the Start*, Boosey & Hawkes

ROWLEY: *Farandole*, Belwin-Mills

ROWLEY: *Scherzo*, Belwin-Mills

SEITZ-KLOTMAN: *Concerto No. 5*, Belwin-Mills (with orchestra accompaniment)

SIENNICKI: *Highland Heather*, Kjos

THIRD POSITION

Album of Classical Pieces, vols. 1, 2, and 3, International Music

BACH-FORBES: *Jesu, Joy of Man's Desiring*, Oxford University Press

BAKER: *Concert Piece for Viola*, MMB

BRUNSON: *Bariolage Badinage*, Kjos

DOCKTOR: *Solos for the Viola Player*, G. Schirmer (Hal Leonard)

FORBES, ed.: *Chester Music for Viola*, Chester Music

GURLITTA: *Scherzino*, Schmidt

HARVEY: *The Viola Player's Repertory*, Ditson

HEACOX: *Ten Easy Solos*, Ditson

MAGANINI: *Concert Album for Viola and Piano*, Edition Musicus

PONCE: *Estrellita*, Carl Fischer

TCHAIKOWSKY: *Chanson Triste*, Carl Fischer

TELEMANN: *Concerto No. 3 in F for 4 Violas*, Boosey & Hawkes

WHISTLER-HUMMEL: *Concert and Contest Album*, Rubank

Collections with Piano Accompaniment

FIRST POSITION

FORBES: *A First-Year Classical Album*, Oxford University Press

KRITCH: *First Book of Viola Pieces*, Witmark

MURRAY-TATE: *Tunes Old and New*, Oxford University Press

NELSON, ed.: *Waggon Wheels*, Boosey & Hawkes

STOUTMAIRE AND HENDERSON: *Duets for All*, Belwin-Mills

SUZUKI: *Viola School, vols. 1-5*, Summy-Birchard Music

34 Viola Solos, Belwin-Mills

WHISTLER: *Solos for Strings* (viola), Rubank

A good book for beginners and individual instruction is Hans Sitt's *Practical Viola Method* (Carl Fischer).

Solo Music for the Cello

FIRST POSITION AND EXTENSIONS

BAY: *Fun with the Cello*, Mel Bay Publishers, Inc.

DEAK: *Autumn Song, and Lullaby*, Belwin-Mills

DOTTLEIN, ed.: *Collection of Small Pieces*, vol. 1, Schott

FLETCHER: *New Tunes for Strings*, vol. 1, Boosey & Hawkes

GOOVEY: *My Cello tunes*, Boosey & Hawkes

HOLLAENDER: *Six Easy Pieces*, Boston Music

KRANE: *Classical and Folk Melodies*, Presser

MOFFAT: *Old Masters for Young Cellists*, Associated Music

NASH: *Prelude, Barcarolle, a Memory*, G. Schirmer

NELSON: *Right from the Start*, Boosey & Hawkes

NELSON: *Stepping Stones*, Boosey & Hawkes

OTIS: *First Book of Study Pieces*, Boston Music

POPEJOY: *Melodious Studies for Cello*, Belwin-Mills

POPEJOY: *The Singing Cello*, Belwin-Mills

RENTMEISTER, ed.: *Easy Violoncello Duets*, C. F. Peters

SQUIRE: *In Dreamland*, Carl Fischer

SUZUKI, ed.: *Suzuki Cello School, vols. 1 and 2*, Birch Tree Group

WHISTLER: *Solos for Strings*, Rubank

FIRST AND FOURTH POSITIONS
AND EXTENSIONS

ALEXANDER: *Southward-Bound Suite*, Associated Music

CORKER: *In Ireland Suite*, Associated Music

GRANT: *Duets for Two Cellos*, Ludwig Music

GRETCHANINOFF: *Early Morn Suite*, Associated Music

HERFURTH: *Classical Album of Early-Grade Pieces*, Boston Music

JARNEFELT: *Berceuse*, Carl Fischer

KRANE: *Bach for the Cello*, G. Schirmer

O'CONNOR: *Serenade*, Shawnee Press, Inc.

SUZUKI, ed.: *Suzuki Cello School*, vols 3–5, Birch Tree Group

TANSMAN: *Nous jouons pour Maman*, Associated Music

FIRST FOUR AND HALF POSITIONS AND EXTENSIONS

BREVAL: *Sonata in C Major*, Associated Music

Cellist's Solo Album, Carl Fischer

CIRRI: *Arioso*, Edition Musicus

DIBIASE: *Reverie*, Carl Fischer

FLETCHER: *New Tunes for Strings*, vol. 2, Boosey & Hawkes

MARTINI: *Gavotte*, G. Schirmer

MENDELSSOHN: *Student Concerto in D*, Carl Fischer (with orchestra accompaniment)

ROMBERG: *Sonata in B Flat, Op. 43, No. 1*, International Music

SCHROEDER: *Easy Violoncello Classics*, Book I, Boston Music

SQUIRE: *Danse Rustique*, Carl Fischer

TICCIATI: *12 Concert Pieces*, Oxford University Press

WEBSTER: *Scherzo*, Boston Music

ADDITIONAL SOLOS FOR THE CELLO

For additional solo material for the cello player, see Louis A. Potter, Jr.'s *Graded List of Materials and Repertoire for Cello*. Extended lists may also be found in the appendix of *The Art of Cello Playing*, by Louis A. Potter, Jr. (Summy-Birchard).

CELLO METHODS

Benoy	*First-Year Cello Method*	Novello (Shawnee Press, Inc.)	E
Benoy and Sutton	*Introduction to Thumb Position on the Cello*	Oxford Univ. Press	M-MD
Deak	*Modern Method for the Violoncello*	Elkan-Vogel, Inc. (Theodore Presser Co.)	
Dotzauer	*Violoncello Method, vol. I*	Carl Fischer	E-ME
Duncan	*Technical Studies for Beginning Cello*	Mel Bay Pub., Inc.	E
Epperson	*The Art of Cello Teaching*	ASTA	
Pinkston and Moore	*Finger Trips for Cello (Introducing the Positions)*	Mel Bay Pub., Inc.	ME-M
Sazar	*New Directions in Cello Playing*	Of Note	M
Smith, G. Jean	*Cellist's Guide to the Core Technique (2nd ed.)*	ASTA	

Solo Music for the String Bass

EASY

BAKALANOVA: *Ten Easy Pieces,* Leeds Music

BAKALEINIKOFF: *Valse,* Belwin-Mills

BRATTON-MacLEAN: *Teddy Bear's Picnic,* Music Publishers Holding Corporation

CARROL: *Five Simple Pieces for the Double Bass,* Augener

DE COURSEY, RALPH: *Six Easy Pieces,* BMI-Canada

DREW: *First Sonatina,* Belwin-Mills

HARTLEY: *Double-Bass Solos, BKI,* Oxford

ISAAC: *Jolly Dutchman,* Carl Fischer

ISAAC: *Nautical Medley, The Jolly Dutchman,* Carl Fischer

LESINSKY: *Thirty-Four String Bass Solos,* Belwin-Mills

MERLE: *Mummers,* Carl Fischer

MONTIVERDI, ZIMMERMAN, ed.: *Six Songs,* MCA

MONOHAN: *Melodic Studies,* Harris (Ontario)

NELSON: *Tetratunes for Double Bass,* Boosey & Hawkes

OSBORNE: *The Really Easy Bass Book,* Faber Music

SCHEMULLER: *Prayer,* Carl Fischer

SCHUMAN-APPLEBAUM: *The Strange Man,* Belwin-Mills

SIENNICKI: *Highland Heather,* Kjos

WALTER: *The Melodious Bass,* MCA

WHISTLER: *Solos for Strings,* Rubank

MEDIUM

ANDERSON A. C.: *Sonatina,* Carl Fischer

BACH-ZIMMERMAN: *Gavotte,* Carl Fisher

BAKALEINIKOFF: *Allegro Moderato,* Belwin-Mills

CIRRI: *Arioso,* Edition Musicus

CORELLI-ZIMMERMAN: *Sarabande,* Carl Fischer

DREW: *Second Sonatina,* Belwin-Mills

GATES, EVERETT: *Night Song,* Boosey & Hawkes

GOSSEC-SKALMER: *Gavotte,* Volkwein

HANDEL-THOMPSON: *Allegro for String Bass,* Carl Fischer

HANDEL-ZIMMERMAN: *Largo,* Jenkins Music

HARTLEY: *Double-Bass Solos,* Bk. II, Oxford

KOHLER: *Two Austrian Folk Tunes,* Belwin-Mills

LESINSKY (Arranger): *34 String-Bass Solos,* Belwin-Mills

MERLE: *Caballero,* Carl Fischer

PURCELL: *Aria,* International Music

THOMPSON: *Bass Faddle,* Carl Fischer

VIVALDI-ZIMMERMAN: *Intermezzo* (from Concerto in D Minor), G. Schirmer

WALTER, DAVID: *The Elephant's Gavotte,* Yorke Edition

MEDIUM-DIFFICULT

CAPUZZI: *Concerto in F,* Boosey & Hawkes

DRAGONETTI, TURETSKY, ed.: *Six Waltzes,* McGinnes & Marx

PERGOLESI-ZIMMERMAN: *The Giorni,* Carl Fischer

MARCELLO: *Sonata in E Minor,* International Music

MARCELLO: *Sonata in F Major,* International Music

MARIE-SEVITZKY: *La Cinquantine,* G. Ricordi

OSTRANDER: *Album for String Bass and Piano,* Edition Musicus

TELEMANN: *Sonata in A Minor,* International Music

ZIMMERMAN: *Bach for the Young Bass Player,* MCA Music

STRING BASS METHODS

Composer-Arranger	Title	Publisher
Curtis	*A Modern Method for String Bass (Jazz Oriented)*	Berklee Press
Dragonetti	*5 Studies*	Carish
Drew, Spinosa, and Rusch	*The Artists Studio for Strings (Bass Books)*	Kjos
Green, Barry	*The Fundamentals of Double Bass Playing*	Piper Co.
Hause	*96 Etudes*	Presser
Kreutzer-Simandl	*18 Studies*	International
Marcelli	*Carl Fischer Basic Method for the String Bass (Books I & II)*	C. Fischer
Protnoi	*Creative Bass Technique*	ASTA
Schwabe	*Scale Studies*	International
Simandl	*New Method for the Double Bass (Books 1 and 2)*	C. Fischer
Zimmerman	*Elementary Double-Bass Method*	Schirmer

Recommended Reading

APPLEBAUM, SAMUEL, and SADA APPLEBAUM. *With the Artists* (series). Neptune, NJ: Paganiaiana Publications, 1958–1985.

AUER, LEOPOLD. *Violin Playing.* Philadelphia: Lippincott, 1960.

BARRETT, HENRY. *The Viola: Complete Guide for Teacher and Students.* Tuscaloosa, AL: The University of Alabama Press, 1978.

BEREUD, MARGARET. *Modern Shifting Studies for the Violin.* Bryn Mawr: Theodore Presser Co., 1982.

BOYDEN, DAVID. *The History of Violin Playing from Its Origins to 1761.* London: Oxford University Press.

DALTON, DAVID. *Playing the Viola: Conversations with William Primrose.* London: Oxford University Press, 1973.

DILLON, JACQUELYN A., and CASIMER KREICHBAUM. *How to Design and Teach a Successful School String and Orchestra Program.* San Diego, CA: Kjos, 1978.

DILLON-KRASS, JACQUELYN, and DOROTHY A. STRAUB. *TIPS: Establishing a String and Orchestra Program.* Reston, VA: Music Educators National Conference, 1991.

EPPERSON, GORDON. *The Art of Cello Teaching.* Bryan Mawr: Presser, American String Teachers Association, 1980.

FLESCH, CARL. *The Art of Violin Playing: Technique in General, Applied Technique.* Book I. New York: Fischer, 1939.

FLESCH, CARL. *The Art of Violin Playing: Artistic Realization and Instruction.* Book II. New York: Fischer, 1930.

GALAMIAN-GREEN. *Principles of Violin Playing and Teaching.* Englewood Cliffs, NJ: Prentice-Hall, 1962.

GIGANTE, CHARLES. *Manual of Orchestral Bowings.* American String Teachers Association, 1986.

GREEN, BARRY. *The Fundamentals of Double-Bass Playing.* Cincinnati, OH: Piper Press, 1971.

GREEN, ELIZABETH A. H. *The Miraculous Teacher: Ivan Galamian and the Meadowmount Experience.* Reston, VA: ASTA, 1993.

GREEN, ELIZABETH A. H. *The Modern Conductor,* Englewood Cliffs, NJ: Prentice Hall, 1981.

GREEN, ELIZABETH A. H. *Orchestral Bowings and Routines.* Reston, VA: ASTA, 1990.

GREEN, ELIZABETH A. H. *Teaching String Instruments in Classes.* Reston, VA: ASTA, 1987.

Guidelines for Performances of School Music Groups. Reston, VA: Music Educators National Conference, 1986.

HAVAS, KATÓ, and JEROME LANDSMAN. *Freedom to Play.* New York: ABI/Alexander Broude, 1981.

HERMANN, EVELYN. *Shinichi Suzuki, the Man and His Philosophy.* Athens, OH: Ability Development, 1981.

HODGSON, PERCIVAL. *Motion Study and Violin Bowing.* Presser, American String Teachers Association, 1983.

JACKSON, BERMAN, and SARCH. *The A.S.T.A. Dictionary of Bowing Terms.* Bryn Mawr: Presser, American String Teachers Association, 1987.

KLOTMAN, ROBERT, CHAIR. *The Complete String Guide.* Reston, VA: ASTA or Music Educators National Conference, 1988.

KROLICK, EDWARD. *Basic Principles of Double-Bass Playing.* Washington, D.C.: Music Educators National Conference, 1959.

LAMB, NORMAN. *Guide to Teaching Strings,* 4th ed. Dubuque, IA: William C. Brown, 1984.

MATESKY and WOMACK. *String Teachers' Handbook for Organizing String Classes.* Sherman Oaks: Alfred, 1970.

MILLS and SUZUKI. *Parents, In the Suzuki Style.* Diablo Press, 1974.

MOZART, LEOPOLD. *Violin Playing.* London: Oxford University Press, 1959.

POTTER JR., LOUIS. *The Art of Cello Playing.* Princeton: Summy-Birchard, 1964.

PRIMROSE, WILLIAM. *Technique Is Memory.* New York: Oxford University Press, 1960.

RABIN, MARVIN, and PRISCILLA SMITH. *Guide to Orchestral Bowings through Musical Styles* (a manual to be used with video). Madison: University of Wisconsin Extension Arts, 1984.

READ, GARDNER. *Thesaurus of Orchestral Devices.* London: Pitman, 1953.

ROLLAND, PAUL. *Basic Principles of Violin Playing.* Washington, D.C.: Music Educators National Conference, 1959.

ROLLAND, PAUL, and MARLA MUTSCHLER. *The Teaching of Action in String Playing.* Champaign-Urbana, IL: Illinois String Research Associates, 1974.

ROSENBERG, FRED. *The Violin, The Technic of Relaxation and Power.* Bryn Mawr: Presser, American String Teachers Association, 1987.

SMITH, G. JEAN. *Cellist's Guide to the Core Technique (2nd ed.),* Reston, VA: ASTA, 1993.

STANTON, DAVID. *The String Double Bass.* Evanston: "The Instrumentalist," 1965.

SZIGETI, JOSEPH. *Szigeti on the Violin.* London: Vassell, 1969.

SZIGETI, JOSEPH. *With Strings Attached.* New York: Knopf, 1961.

YOUNG, PHYLLIS. *Playing the String Game.* Austin: University of Texas Press, 1978.

YOUNG, PHYLLIS. *String Play: The Drama of Playing and Teaching Strings.* Austin: University of Texas Press, 1978.

ZURFLUH, JOHN D., ed. *Stringed Instrument Repair and Maintenance Manual.* Reston, VA: ASTA, 1978.

Selected readings from *The Strad,* published by J. H. Lavender and Co., 2 Duncan Terrace, London, N. I.

Published lists and bulletins by the Music Educators National Conference and the American String Teachers Association.

String Instrument Inspection Record

The care-and-maintenance list that follows was prepared by Dr. Paul Van Bodegraven, formerly chairman of the Department of Music, New York University, and was first published by the Educational Division of Scherl & Roth, Inc. It is a valuable aid to potential string teachers in determining whether instruments are in the best possible playing condition. It has been expanded by this author. All answers should be "yes."

A. PEGS

	Yes	No
1. Do they fit snugly in both peg-hole openings?	☐	☐
2. Do they turn smoothly and silently?	☐	☐
3. Do they hold in position with slight inward pressure when turned?	☐	☐

B. FINGERBOARD NUT

	Yes	No
1. Do all strings clear the fingerboard without buzzing when playing open or stopped strings?	☐	☐
2. Are the string grooves in the fingerboard nut shallow?	☐	☐

C. FINGERBOARD

	Yes	No
1. Is it smooth with no grooves?	☐	☐
2. Is it glued securely onto the neck?	☐	☐
3. Is it free of excess glue along edges?	☐	☐
4. Is it the proper height?	☐	☐
5. Has it been wiped clean?	☐	☐

D. BRIDGE

	Yes	No
1. Is it the proper height?	☐	☐
2. Do the feet fit perfectly with the top contour?	☐	☐
3. Is the E string on the low side of violin bridge, A string on viola and cello, G string on bass?	☐	☐
4. Is it set opposite the inside notches on the F holes?	☐	☐
5. Are all string grooves shallow?	☐	☐
6. Is it perfectly straight, not warped?	☐	☐
7. Does it lean slightly towards the tailpiece?	☐	☐
8. Is there sufficient arch so that the student does not have difficulty playing from one string to the other?	☐	☐

E. TAILPIECE

	Yes	No
1. Is the small end of tailpiece almost even with the outside edge of saddle?	☐	☐
2. Is there some space between it and top of instrument?	☐	☐
3. Is there a clearance between tailpiece and chinrest?	☐	☐

F. STRINGS

	Yes	No
1. Are all perfectly smooth, without kinks?	☐	☐
2. Is the metal winding tight?	☐	☐
3. Are the adjusters on all metal strings working smoothly?	☐	☐
4. Are the strings free of caked rosin?	☐	☐
5. Do you have an extra set of strings in your case?	☐	☐
6. Are your reserve strings sealed from dryness?	☐	☐
7. If you have any steel strings on your instrument, are they equipped with adjusters?	☐	☐

8. Have you checked to be sure that the strings are not false? ☐ ☐
9. Are the strings wound straight on all pegs? ☐ ☐

G. INSTRUMENT BODY

1. Is it free from open cracks? ☐ ☐
2. Is the top clean and free of caked rosin? ☐ ☐
3. Are the front and back thoroughly glued to the ribs? ☐ ☐

H. THE SOUNDPOST

1. Is it directly behind the right foot of the bridge? ☐ ☐
2. Is it perpendicular to top and back? ☐ ☐
3. Is the soundpost-setter slot facing the right F hole? ☐ ☐

I. THE BOW

1. Can it be loosened and tightened freely? ☐ ☐
2. Does it have enough hair? ☐ ☐
3. Does the hair extend the full width of the frog ferrule? ☐ ☐
4. Has it been rehaired in the past year? ☐ ☐
5. Is the bow stick free of caked rosin? ☐ ☐
6. Does it have real wire winding and leather thumb grip? ☐ ☐
7. Is the bow arch noticeable and not warped when it is tightened
   ready to play? ☐ ☐
8. Is there a protective facing, ivory or metal, on the tip? ☐ ☐
9. Is the frog free from cracks? ☐ ☐

J. CHIN REST

1. Is the chin rest securely attached to instrument? ☐ ☐
2. Is the chin rest free of broken edges? ☐ ☐
3. Is it of proper height for correct posture and comfortable playing? ☐ ☐

K. ROSIN

1. Do you have a full-size (unbroken) cake of rosin? ☐ ☐
2. Do you have a clean cake of rosin? ☐ ☐
3. Are you using rosin for the individual bow, that is, violin, cello,
   or bass rosin? ☐ ☐

L. MUTE

1. Do you have a mute available, ready for instant use? ☐ ☐

M. CELLO AND BASSES

1. Is the adjustable endpin in proper working order? ☐ ☐
2. Do you have a cello or bass endpin rest that prevents instrument
   slipping while playing? ☐ ☐

Repairing String Instruments

Repairing a string instrument requires a skilled, knowledgeable repairman. Maintenance, however, can be done by any concerned, responsible individual who is willing to take the time to acquire information regarding a few simple procedures. In addition there are some minor repairs that a teacher can do to help the student through a critical moment.

It is important, however, that teachers realize that there are limitations to what they can repair even under emergency situations. When such a situation occurs, they should leave these repairs to a reputable repairman. Too often serious damage has been done to string instruments by uninformed, well-intentioned, amateur repair persons.

PROPER ADJUSTMENT

It is important that string instruments be in good working condition (properly adjusted) for the following reasons:

1. Proper adjustment provides for a better sound.
2. When the instrument is out of adjustment, students become frustrated by the handicaps created. Proper adjustment facilitates playing.
3. When playing is made easier and sounds better, a student's pride and confidence in performing increases.

MINOR REPAIRS

When a string breaks, follow these procedures:

1. Loop it through the hole in the tail piece or hook it to the tuner.
2. Place the opposite end through the opening in the appropriate peg, and wind the string so that the winding moves toward the wall of the peg box and does *not* cross another string.
3. If a metal string is being used, be certain that the bridge pad (protector) is in the groove in order to prevent the string from cutting into the bridge.

Replacing a bridge requires a great deal of skill and knowledge. Following are a few rules that might be helpful in an emergency:

1. *Never* glue the feet of the bridge to the top of the violin.
2. Try and find a bridge that matches the height of the broken bridge. It is imperative that the bridge not be too high or too low. (When the bridge is assembled, test it by feeling; try playing a few notes.)
3. To have the feet fit the top properly, put a piece of fine sandpaper on the top, under the place where the feet of the bridge will go, *with the abrasive side up* facing the bridge. Then gently rub the feet on the sand-

paper at the appropriate spot so that the paper sands the feet until they fit the top of the violin snugly. Match the grooves with the broken bridge before cutting the notches. When assembling the bridge with the violin and strings, be certain that the *high* side is under the G string. Tilt the bridge slightly back toward the tailpiece so that the pressure from the strings is focused on the center of the bridge.

A warped bridge must be replaced. However, a temporary solution is to soak it in water over night. Allow it to dry *standing* so that it will get air from all sides.

If the bridge is too low, it can be raised by placing a small piece of cardboard under each foot. If it is too high, remove some wood from the top edge and then make new grooves. "Also, make sure the string notches are only 1/3 of the string thickness deep."[1]

Miscellaneous parts that can be handled easily:

1. If tailgut breaks, keep a supply of Sacconi tailguts on hand. They can be screwed on and adjusted to length easily and quickly.
2. Stock tuners for emergency replacements.
3. Keep a chin-rest key on hand at all times to tighten chin rests when they become loose and fall off.
4. If using Caspari pegs, keep a key handy to tighten the screw in pegs.

In an emergency some corrections can be made to secure proper bowhair tension.

1. If the hair is too long, put some cardboard under the hair at the tip so that it will increase the tension. This is only a temporary solution.
2. If the hair is too short, wet the hair and pull two equally divided parts of hair around the stick and to the back. Brace the hair and hold it in place with a small object like a toothpick. Be certain to wrap something like string around the tip to make it secure and prevent it from breaking.
3. If the eyelet thread becomes stripped, pinch it with pliers just enough to make the screw work.
4. When the button comes off, melt some rosin and put it in the hole. Then insert the screw.
5. Wash dirty hair in very soapy water with a toothbrush and hang it to dry.

MAJOR REPAIRS

These should be done entirely by a professional repairman.

1. Cracks in the body of the instrument are caused by stress. Find the source.
2. Gluing the fingerboard or adjusting the height and curvature by planning should not be done by the uninitiated.

[1]Horn, Peter, *Emergency Repair Manual.* Cleveland: Horn and Son Stringed Instruments, 2570 Superior Avenue, Cleveland, Ohio 44114.

3. Bow rehairing needs a professional hand.

4. Adjusting the sound post requires a sound-post adjuster and expert knowledge regarding placement and its affect on tone.

FACTORS AFFECTING AN INSTRUMENT'S TONE

1. A bow that needs rehairing results in a glassy, sliding sound.

2. Improper adjustment and not having the sound post in its most productive position can cause difficulties in playing as well as affect tone. These factors will vary from instrument to instrument.

3. The quality of the instrument is important. This does not mean that a student needs the best instrument, but it does imply that there is a point of diminishing return when purchases are based entirely on cost.

A String Teacher's Emergency Box

One of the most costly expenses for a board of education—and a source of frustration to string teachers whose teaching may be interrupted—are minor failures in equipment. To remedy this situation, string teachers, especially traveling teachers, are advised to have on hand ASTA's *Stringed Instrument Repair and Maintenance Manual* and a portable equipment box that contains the following items:

1. Multiple sets of strings for all of the instruments;
2. A chin-rest key to tighten or attach loose chin rests;
3. Peg compound;
4. Tweezers and pliers;
5. Rosin for violin/viola, cello, and string bass;
6. Tail gut (Sacconi tail gut has grooved ends to facilitate repairs);
7. A polishing cloth;
8. Rubber bands;
9. Foam rubber for shoulder-pad insulation on violins and violas; and
10. Extra end pin blocks for the cello and string bass.

Fingering Charts

Violin

*Beginning with the second position, accidentals are omitted so that the chart can be followed more easily. A rule to follow in the beginning is that accidentals generally use the same finger, raised or lowered, as an uninflected note. Examples:

*Beginning with the second position, accidentals are omitted so that the chart can be followed more easily. A rule to follow in the beginning is that accidentals generally use the same finger, raised or lowered, as an uninflected note. Examples:

Violoncello

THUMB POSITION

At the seventh position, the cellist has reached the point of maximum reach for the hand. He then employs the thumb position. The thumb is placed where the first finger was located in seventh position, one octave above the open string. The sign for the use of the thumb is ♀. The thumb position uses both the tenor and the treble clefs. The following is the fingering for the D-major scale in thumb position:

*Beginning with the fifth position, not all accidentals are included. The chart is merely a guide; the intervals determine the correct relationships in finger placement.

String Bass

Publishers, Music Dealers, and Other Resources

Alfred Publishing Co., Inc.
16380 Roscoe Blvd.
P. O. Box 10003
Van Nuys, CA 91410-0008

American String Teachers Association
1806 Robert Fulton Drive, Suite 300
Reston, VA 22091

Belwin-Mills (Warner Bros.)
15800 N. W. 48th Avenue
Miami, FL 33014

Boosey & Hawkes, Inc.
24 East 21st Street
New York, NY 10010-7200

Glaesel
Orchestral Instruments
The Selmer Company, Inc.
P. O. Box 310
Elkhart, IN 46515-0310

Hal Leonard Publishing Corporation
P. O. Box 13819
7777 W. Blue Mound Road
Milwaukee, WI 53213

Highland/Etling Publishing Co.
(See Alfred)

Kalmus
c/o Warner Brothers Publications, Inc.
15800 N.W. 48th Ave.
Miami, FL 33014

Neil A. Kjos Music Co. Publishers
4380 Jutland Drive
San Diego, CA 92117-0894

Mel Bay Publications, Inc.
P. O. Box 66
4 Industrial Drive
Pacific, MO 63069-0066

Scherl & Roth
United Musical Instruments USA, Inc.
P. O. Box 727
Elkhart, IN 46515

Shar Products Company
P. O. Box 1411
Ann Arbor, MI 48106

Southern Music Co.
P. O. Box 329
1100 Broadway
San Antonio, TX 78292

Southwestern Stringed Instruments
and Accessories
1228 E. Prince Rd.
Tucson, AZ 85719

Stanton's Sheet Music
330 S. Fourth St.
Columbus, OH 43215

Summy-Birchard, Inc.
c/o Warner Brothers Publications, Inc.
15800 N.W. 48th Ave.
Miami, FL 33014

Super-Sensitive Musical String Co.
6121 Porter Rd.
Sarasota, FL 34240-9542

Sweetwater Sounds, Inc.
5335 Bass Rd.
Fort Wayne, IN 46808

Wm. Lewis and Son
300 Marcus Ave., Suite 2W7
Lake Success, NY 10042

Zeta Music Systems, Inc.
2230 Livingston
Oakland, CA 94606

Professional Organizations

American String Teachers Association
1806 Robert Fulton Drive, Suite 300
Reston, VA 22091

Chamber Music America
545 Eighth Ave.
New York, NY 10018

Music Educators National
Conference
1806 Robert Fulton Dr.
Reston, VA 22091-4348

National School Orchestra
Association
Starkville High School
801 Louisville Rd.
Starkville, MS 39759-3799

Suzuki Association of the Americas
P. O. Box 17310
Boulder, CO 80308

Glossary for Strings

The American String Teachers Association has published the comprehensive *Dictionary of Bowing and Pizzicato Terms*, by Barbara Seagrave, Joel Berman, and Kenneth Sarch. It may be obtained from ASTA in Reston, Virginia.

A due corde (It.), upon two strings
Allonger l'archet (Fr.), lengthen the bow stroke
A punta d'arco (It.), at the point of the bow
Arco (It.), use the bow
Arpeggio (It.), notes of a chord played in broken fashion
A una corda (It.), on one string
Bogen (Ger.), violin bow
Coll'arco (It.), play with the bow

Collé, a bowing in which the string is pinched lightly, followed by a lift to prepare for the next stroke (see p. 194)
Col legno (It.), with the wood part of the bow (see p. 191)
Con sordini (It.), with mutes
Corda (It.), string
Cordatura (It.), the notes to which the strings, any strings, are tuned

Coup d'archet (Fr.), stroke of the bow

Détaché (Fr.), literally "detached"—any form of separated bowing on the string (see p. 181)

Down-bow, sign is ⊓ the bow is drawn from the hand away from the instrument

Double stop, playing simultaneously on two strings (see p. 90)

Due corde (It.), two strings

Flautando (It.), light, airy; played over the fingerboard

Frog, the lower end of the bow, to which the hair is fastened

Glissando (It.), slide the fingers in gliding manner

Head, point of the violin bow

Legato (It.), smooth or sometimes tied together (⌒)

Leggiero (It.), light, delicate

Legno (It.), wood or stick part of the bow (see p. 191)

Lever l'archet (Fr.), lift the bow

Louré (Fr.), bowing style for pulsed or legato notes (see p. 189)

Marcato (It.), refers to an accentuated or well-marked style of bowing

Martelé (Fr.), hammered or sharply accented style of bowing (see p. 185)

Mettez la sourdine (Fr.), put on the mute

Mute, a small clamp made of various metals or wood that is placed on the bridge to dampen the sound of the instrument

Neck, that part of a string instrument extending from the head to the body; the fingerboard is attached to it

Nut, the small bridge at the upper end of the fingerboard over which the strings pass into the peg box; sometimes it is used synonymously with the frog

Parlando (It.), in a declamatory style, using a variety of expressive bowings as if "to speak"

Piqué (Fr.), a martelé style of bowing at the tip

Pointe (Fr.), tip of the bow

Ponticello (It.), bow close to the bridge to produce a "squeaky" effect (see p. 190)

Portato (It.), see Louré

Portamento (It.), gliding effect from note to note for expressive purposes

Pt., the point of the bow

Punta (It.), the point or bow tip

Ricochet (Fr.), a bouncing style of bowing that involves two or more slurred notes; the bow is dropped on the string so that it ricochets

Saltando (It.), leaping, skipping the bow—a bouncing bow

Sans sourdine (Fr.), without a mute

Sautillé (Fr.), a rapid bouncing bow that occurs through the natural resiliency of the stick

Scordatura (It.), a special tuning of the open strings (see p. 195)

Slurred, two or more notes indicated by a ⌒ and played in a smooth manner, moving in the same direction

Sordino (It.), mute

Spiccato (It.), a bouncing bow indicated by a dot over the note (see p. 186)

Staccato (It.), detached and distinctly separated bowing (see p. 182)

Sul tasto (It.), over the fingerboard (see p. 192)

Tip, head of the bow

Tremolo (It.), a note or chord reiterated at a rapid rate; it may or may not be measured (see p. 187)

U.H., upper half of the bow

Una corda (It.), on one string only

Up-bow, the sign is V; start at the point of the bow and move the hand toward the instrument

W.B., whole bow

Index